Ideology and
Caribbean
Integration

P1-12

31-48

other 9-44

49-100

CONSORTIUM GRADUATE SCHOOL OF SOCIAL SCIENCES
NEW GENERATION SERIES
Norman Girvan, Series Editor
Bill Riviere, Associate Series Editor

This series brings to the attention of academic readers and the general public the work of young Caribbean scholars on a broad range of topics related to Caribbean development, orginally undertaken for research degrees at the Consortium Graduate School.

ACKNOWLEDGEMENTS

Research by students at the Consortium Graduate School of Social Sciences has been supported by grants from the International Development Research Centre.

The School's programme has also received support from the United Nations Development Programme, UNESCO, the Ford Foundation, and the Commonwealth Fund for Technical Cooperation.

The New Generation Series of publications is supported by a grant from the Caribbean Development Bank.

Ideology
and
Caribbean
Integration

Ian Boxill

**with an Introduction
by the Hon. William G. Demas**

This was on his thesis

Consortium Graduate School of Social Sciences
UNIVERSITY OF THE WEST INDIES
MONA   JAMAICA

The Consortium Graduate School of Social Sciences
University of the West Indies
Mona   Kingston 7   Jamaica
ISBN 976-41-0045-7
ISSN 0799-0057

in collaboration with Canoe Press University of the West Indies
Barbados · Jamaica · Trinidad and Tobago

This title in the New Generation Series has been
published with financial assistance from the
Caribbean Development Bank

01   00   99   98   97   5   4   3   2

NATIONAL LIBRARY OF JAMAICA
CATALOGUING IN PUBLICATION DATA

Boxill, Ian
     Ideology and Caribbean integration

     p. cm. — (New generation series)
     Bibliography : p.
     ISBN 976-41-0045-7
     1. Caribbean Community countries.
     2. Regionalism – Caribbean, English-speaking.
     I. Title. II. Series.
     337.1729 – dc 20

Book design by Orville Bloise
Set in 10.5 x 13 Times x 27

To my mother and father,
Costella and Samuel Boxill,
two of the most genuine regionalists
I have ever known.
Also to William Demas,
a man ever faithful
the the regionalist idea

Contents

List of Illustrations

Figures

List of Tables

xi

Foreword 1993

The Consortium Graduate School of Social Sciences is pleased to present *Ideology and Regional Integration* by Ian Boxill, the first title in its **New Generation Series** of publications. This Series, produced in collaboration with Canoe Press, University of the West Indies, will be based initially on Ph.D. and M.Phil. theses prepared by students at the School. It aims to bring to the attention of academic readers and the general public the work of young Caribbean scholars on a variety of subjects of historical interest and policy relevance to the region.

Boxill's monograph comes against the background of the persistent failure to consolidate a strong Caribbean Community as envisioned by the Treaty of Chaguaramas, and the poor record of implementation by the governments of member states of decisions taken at the CARICOM level. This "implementation gap" has become a major source of disappointment and frustration with the integration movement, and has contributed to widespread cynicism amongst the public of the region. The last major attempt to restart the momentum of the CARICOM process was the far-reaching set of recommendations contained in *Time for Action,* the report of the independent West Indian Commission which worked in 1991-92. Nevertheless, there has been a paucity of independent analysis of the underlying factors which explain CARICOM's problematic record of achievements.

Boxill's work is a much needed contribution in this area. Its principal proposition is that the weakness and instability of the integration movement can be attributed to the absence of a coherent ideology of regionalism. He argues that the record shows that member states have not shown an overriding commitment to regionalism as an end in itself. Analysis of the actions of governments in the areas of trade and foreign policy suggests that regionalism is used in an opportunistic manner, when it is seen as instrumental for the pursuit of specific objectives. When a member state perceives that it can achieve its national goals through independent action, regionalism is forgotten. This fundamental weakness is reflected in the pragmatic conceptual and institutional framework of the Community arising out of the provisions of the Treaty of Chaguaramas, which allows member states to opt in or out of regionalist actions depending on their interests and circumstances.

Boxill further supports these arguments by the findings of a survey of elitist attitudes conducted in Jamaica and St. Lucia. These suggest that what exists in the region is less a regional ideology and more a regional orientation or ideation; that this tendency is stronger in St. Lucia than in Jamaica; and that it is weaker among the economic elite than the political and cultural elite in the two countries.

Boxill goes further to make specific recommendations about how an ideology of regionalism can be developed. However, I question how far such an ideology can command widespread acceptance in the absence of a solid economic foundation showing that regionalism corresponds to the material interests of the dominant economic players, and the majority classes, in the Caribbean. The principal economic processes of CARICOM countries are still centered on the trading and financial linkages with North America and Western Europe. This is reflected in the preoccupations of governments and the perceived interests of businessmen and investors.

Hence, development of a regionalist ideology mainly on a political and cultural basis will have to contend with the dissonance of the economic sphere. Unfortunately, attempts to provide an economic rationale to the regional integration movement have not so far been sufficiently convincing to win the commitment of a substantial section of the business community, and to engage the political will of the governments. Boxill's work points us in the direction of this formidable challenge.

DIRECTOR
CONSORTIUM GRADUATE SCHOOL OF SOCIAL SCIENCES

NORMAN GIRVAN
PROFESSOR

Preface 1996

Since the publication of this book in 1993, a number of important developments have taken place within the regional integration movement. In general, these changes appear to support rather than bring into question the basic argument of this book.

One of the important developments is the implementation of a number of recommendations of the West Indian Commission Report, *Time for Action*, by CARICOM Heads. The West Indian Commission was set up by CARICOM Heads to "formulate proposals for advancing the goals of the Treaty of Chaguaramas which established the Caribbean Community and Common Market (CARICOM) in 1973" (*Time For Action* 1992: 4). In much broader terms the Commission was mandated to come up with a vision to usher the region into the twenty-first century.

Essentially, the report addresses a number of developmental issues and identifies various ways in which to broaden and widen the regional movement. To such an end the Report argues that the creation of a single market and economy, an idea already adopted by CARICOM Heads, is critical to the process of deepening. However, it also suggests, implicitly, that such a goal will not be achieved outside of some common ideological framework, as I argue in this book. The Report's recommendations in this regard are inspired by the opening paragraph of the 1982 'Wise Men' Commission, *The Caribbean Community in the 1980s*, which states:

> ... Caribbean regionalism is the outgrowth of more than 300 years of West Indian Kinship – the vagaries of the socio-economic and political history of transplanted people from which is evolving a Caribbean

identity. Without that element of West Indian identity a Community of Caribbean would be mere markings on parchment – a community without a soul, without a vision, without a shared destiny ... (Quoted in *Time For Action* 1992: 468).

Consistent with this sentiment, the need to proceed within an ideological framework which reproduces the integration process, the Report argues: "We cannot, for example, journey to a Single Market and Economy with a mind-set that looks askance at investment that comes from other parts of CARICOM ... We cannot talk 'community' and treat community partners as 'foreigners'" (*Time For Action* 1992: 469).

To be sure, many of the recommendations of the Report to deepen the process (*eg* free movement of people, cultural and economic cooperation) are also in keeping with the basic tenor of this book.

Nonetheless, although CARICOM Heads have agreed in principle to the idea of a Single Market and Economy, the realisation of the idea still seems a very long way off. Part of the reason lies in fact that nation states in the region continue to subordinate larger regional concerns to much narrower national interests. For instance, freedom of movement legislation is difficult to pass in many countries because it might well have repercussions for electoral outcomes. Hence, few governments are even willing to raise the matter so that there can be some reasoned public debate over the issue. Unfortunately, despite areas of progress, CARICOM remains a movement faced by lack of implementation and sometimes contradictory developmental visions.

As far as the widening process is concerned there has been the inauguration of the Association of Caribbean States (ACS) in 1995. The ACS, which is headquartered in Trinidad and Tobago, represents an attempt by CARICOM to move closer to the non-CARICOM nations in the region. The ACS emerged out of economic and political imperatives – the need for more trade in the face of competing economic blocs, and the creation of alliances with larger countries within the region. The formation of the North American Free Trade Association (NAFTA), European Union and the World Trade Organisation have, by implication, hastened the decision by CARICOM members to expand trading links to embrace larger Caribbean nations. According to the Report:

We see this Association of Caribbean States as being functionally active in an integration sense ...We believe that it should be the means of our creating within the wider Caribbean special trading and functional cooperation arrangements on terms to be negotiated – terms which will recognise the relative weakness of CARICOM economies in relation to some larger partners like Cuba and the

Dominican Republic, Puerto Rico and Venezuela (*Time For Action* 1992: 446-47).

The Report further states: "The Association of Caribbean States could be a vehicle through which other special arrangements could be promoted for the expanding of trade between CARICOM and other countries, or cooperating groups of countries, in the wider Caribbean including the littoral" (*Time For Action*, 1992: 447).

The formation of the ACS is not, therefore, an attempt to dissolve CARICOM nor to diminish its community character. At any rate, there is no reason why CARICOM and the ACS cannot function as two separate but complementary movements. In so far as CARICOM remains the bedrock of the regional integration movement, then analyses which seek to constructively address its weaknesses are still necessary. It is in this context that I believe the ideas contained in this book remain relevant.

This book has not been without criticism, some of them valid, others, unfortunately, based on a very limited reading of the material. Arguably, the most widely made criticism is that I ignored the importance of economic factors in promoting the integration process. Nothing can be further from the truth. In chapter 2, I argue that both material and non-material factors are important if the integration process is to be a success. Nevertheless, although ideology is the glue which holds the process together most of the literature on integration has tended to emphasise the role of economic factors. Therefore, part of the rationale for writing this book had to do with filling the gap in the area of non-material aspects of integration. If it seems that I have over-emphasised the role of non-material factors it may be due to the need I saw to put this issue high on the agenda of discourses on the integration project.

Finally, this book has also attracted positive comments from readers and is now part of the reading material of a significant number of educational and research institutions in the region and across the world. The decision to have a second impression is testimony to the popularity of the subject matter with which it deals, if not the persuasiveness of the argument it makes. Therefore, I have made minor changes to the text. Consequently, this edition departs very little from the first one.

SEPTEMBER 1996

Acknowledgements

This work has benefitted greatly from the input of a number of people. I would like to thank Norman Girvan and the Consortium Graduate School of Social Sciences for providing the opportunity to have this study published. Professor Girvan also contributed to the development of many of the ideas contained in this work. Also, I would like to extend my appreciation to Peter Phillips whose thought provoking comments and criticisms helped me to refine many of my ideas. Thanks should also be extended to Dillon Alleyne, Noel Gray and Michael Heslop for engaging me in debates about many of the issues raised in this study. For suggesting areas of revision I wish to extend my appreciation to Charles Mills and, in particular, Neville Duncan. To William Demas I extend my thanks for his willingness to share his ideas and experiences with me. Other persons who should be mentioned for their contribution include Edward Greene, Keith Hart, C.Y. Thomas, Barry Chevannes, Don Robothom, Rupert Lewis, Bill Riviere, Robert Buddan, Wilbern Persaud, Ronny Turner, the late Carl Stone and the late Derek Gordon.

I am grateful to the politicians, business-persons, managers, journalists, artistes, teachers and public servants in both Jamaica and St. Lucia who kindly gave of their time for interviews. To all of the above, and to those whom I may have overlooked, I would like to say that this work is as much yours as it is mine.

Introduction 1996

by the Hon. William G. Demas

I am pleased to have been asked to write this Introduction to Ian Boxill's *Ideology and Caribbean Integration*. In many ways it is a pioneering effort and indeed a landmark in the study of Caribbean integration. It should be noted that in the book the term integration is used and is not qualified by the term 'political' or 'economic'. It refers to either or to both. In this introduction, however, we shall discuss political and economic integration separately.

To put the book in proper perspective, we need to look at the various attempts in the past to study the question.

Let us first consider briefly political integration. Boxill reminds us that throughout the nineteenth century and the first few decades of this century, the rationale of the British Colonial Office for West Indian political unity was to save on the administrative costs of governing each island separately. On the other hand, in the twentieth century West Indian leaders up to 1960 or so saw Federation, as the author also points out, as an essential step towards West Indian self-government, subsequently referred to as political independence. This rationale rested on the belief that each island (even Jamaica and Trinidad) was too small to proceed to independence by itself – really a variation and an extension of the Colonial Office 'administrative economies' argument. But it went further and there was an 'ideological' element in it – namely, that West Indians were basically one people with a common history, common identity and a single destiny.

But Arthur Lewis and Eric Williams in the 1940s and 1950s stressed another element – the widening of the market for industrial production and (in the case of Williams) some kind of 'rational' allocation of economic activities. Underlying the approaches of these two men there was, too, a strong sentiment of West Indian 'oneness'.

Let us now turn to the purely economic integration aspect. As was to be expected, the arguments for this were at first almost totally economic. They focussed on the wider market, freedom of movement of capital and labour, some joint decision making on the location of industrial and, in some cases, agricultural production.

Between 1960 and the early 1980s the pre and post federal approach by West Indian economists to economic integration did not rest on the 'neo-classical' analysis of Viner, Meade, Balasse *et al.* It rather reflected a more 'protectionist', dynamic and 'economies of scale' rationale for Caribbean economic integration. In an article published in *Social and Economic Studies* (March 1960), I openly attacked the 'trade creation and diversion' approach of the neo-classical economists in the developed countries and argued that just as (a moderate degree of) protection could offer medium and long-term benefits to a country, so could 'trade diversion' have similar benefits in a similar time period in economic groupings of developing countries. In that same article I advocated both an 'inward-looking' (or regional import substitution) and an 'outward-looking' (or extra-regional export promotion) approach to West Indian economic integration, in contrast to a solely 'outward-looking' approach of the neoclassical economists. I was in favour of joint efforts to influence industrial location in any economic integration attempt in the West Indies. These points were further developed in a 1965 book, *The Economics of Development in Small Countries*, and in a 1966 paper, "Planning and the Price-Mechanism in the Context of Caribbean Economic Integration" presented to the Caribbean Scholars' Association Meeting of that year in Guyana.

The matter was carried further in 1965 by Alister McIntyre in his path-breaking paper "Trade Policy and Caribbean Economic Integration", where he not only completely demolished the 'trade diversion' approach of the neoclassicals but also put forward the seminal idea of 'resource combination' that is to say, 'combining' physical imputs from different Caribbean countries to produce *within the region* a more highly processed product for either import substitution or export outside the region.

It was essentially McIntyre's idea of 'resource combination' that served as the basis for the approach taken in the well-known 1967 work of Brewster and Thomas, *The Dynamics of West Indian Integration* where the term 'integration of production' instead of 'resource combination' was used. Norman Girvan and Owen Jefferson also no doubt drew on the basic idea of 'resource combination' when they argued in the late 1960s in *Corporate vs Caribbean Integration* that the transnational corporations were operating in Latin America and the Caribbean to frustrate the integration of production within the latter group of countries.

While none of these post-1960 writers on West Indian economic integration ever wrote about the ideological aspects of the subject from my own personal knowledge of them, I know that they always had a deep commitment to West Indian unity, and that it is very likely that it was their 'ideological' commitment that gave them the impetus to think creatively about the economic integration of our region.

By 1985, as a result of the rise to supremacy of the neoliberal paradigm (a more extreme and dogmatic form of the neoclassical doctrine) in economics in both the developed and the developing countries, the governments of the CARICOM countries now on balance see the economic aspects of CARICOM as resting largely on the integration of the product and factor markets and on monetary integration (rather than on the integration of production), or on regional industrial programming, or on joint development of natural resources, or on rationalization of agriculture in the region. In addition, some crucial decisions have to be taken soon; these all relate to trade and economic agreements with a large number of groups such as the European Union (EU), the Free Trade Area of the Americas (FTAA), the North American Free Trade Association (NAFTA) and other independent countries in the Caribbean archipelago. Much wisdom, vision and judgement have to be exercised in determining what sorts of linkages are useful for the region, and in the sequencing of negotiations. For, what is negotiated with one group is almost certain to have an impact on negotiations with the other group. Much technical preparation will be required for all of the negotiations. Above all, the issue of reciprocity in tariffs and other economic concessions is likely to be of fundamental importance to all negotiations and outcomes. We will be virtually shaping our political and economic futures for the first two or three decades of the twenty-first century. For my part, I am prepared to concede that market integration (and the use of a moderate rather than an excessively high common external tariff) is important because of our need to become more internationally competitive. Now this is where Boxill's point comes in.

For, even under market integration, in order to give sufficient motivation to all the thinkers, policy makers and actors in the regional economic integration movements, there must be some very deep sense of commitment to the region to overcome all the frictions and sense (if not reality) of unequal benefits inherent in the integration process among developing countries; and to think of the need for cohesion, solidarity and self-determination of the region. This deep sense of commitment to the West Indies Boxill terms the 'ideology of regionalism'. He surely is right about the need for such an ideology. This is an important but hitherto underplayed factor in West Indian and indeed Caribbean archipelago economic integration. Apart from emphasising this dimension without neglecting at the theoretical and conceptual level, Boxill makes a bold attempt to measure the 'ideological' aspect at the empirical level in two CARICOM countries. I am sure that this book will be of interest to West Indian and non-West Indian readers and that other scholars will follow in his footsteps in exploring this important dimension of integration.

INSTITUTE OF SOCIAL AND ECONOMIC RESEARCH
UNIVERSITY OF THE WEST INDIES
MONA, JAMAICA

SEPTEMBER 1996

The Honourable William G. Demas, one of the architects of CARICOM, was former Secretary General of CARICOM, former President of the Caribbean Development Bank and former Governor of the Central Bank of Trinidad and Tobago. He was formerly Director of the Andrew Mellon Foundation Project, ISER, Jamaica, and is now Distinguished Research Fellow of the Caribbean Centre for Monetary Studies, St Augustine, Trinidad and Tobago.

CHAPTER 1

Introduction

Over the past decade regional integration movements in the Third World have been undergoing tremendous pressure as they attempt to sustain viability. The Caribbean Community (CARICOM) is no exception. Since the mid 1970s, so serious have some of these difficulties been that practitioners and analysts of regional integration have indicated their doubts about the viability of the regional movement (Hippolyte-Manigat 1979). Among them was Alister McIntyre, a former Secretary General of CARICOM and a leading exponent of Caribbean integration, who stated, in 1983, that it was important to recognize that the integration movement was going through a crisis (McIntrye 1984). McIntyre's comments were firmly rooted in the reality which manifested a decline in intra-regional trade and ever-present trade wars between member countries; conflict over foreign policy formulation and implementation; and an apparent predisposition for member countries to continually breach collective agreements. Indeed, since 1983 there has been little change in the situation to which McIntyre alluded (Samuel 1987).

Against this background, attempts have been made to seek explanations for the difficulties which continue to plague the regional movement. Some of these explanations include emphasis on the presence of too many barriers to trade and poor economic management; lack of political will amongst regional actors; and national economic conflicts exacerbated by crises within the world economy. While these explanations have been, generally, enlightening both in terms of their contribution to knowledge and their ability to offer solutions, most of them have suffered analytically because of their restrictive theoretical framework. On the other hand, those which have been able to escape the limitations imposed by neo-functionalist approaches have failed to pay sufficient attention to the role of the superstructure in the integration process. The major weakness of writings adopting neo-functionalist approaches is their inability to deal adequately with elements of the superstructure, such as values and ideologies, in their analyses of the regional integration process. For instance, neo-functionalist theory has long supported the view that countries which came together in a grouping for economic integration, functional co-operation and sometimes co-ordination of foreign policies would gradually, over time, deepen their inter-relationships, thus ultimately leading to political integration (Demas 1987). Hence, there is great concern with technical issues, such as the harmonization of tariffs and the provision of administrative institutions to facilitate co-operation in areas such as health, education and so on. However, such a view is inconsistent with the experiences of the regional integration movements. According to Demas:

> Experience has shown that this is never so. What has emerged from the experience [of the integration movements] is the conclusion that — particularly in developing countries — political integration, far from being the end product of successful integration in other areas, is really after a certain point, a condition of further deepening of economic, functional and foreign policy integration (Demas 1987:2).

What the neo-functionalist theorists ignore is the fact that cohesion and increased interaction among states also depend on a whole gamut of factors, especially cultural and ideological ones (Hansen 1972).

Neo-functionalist approaches also emphasize economic pragmatism as a basis for integration. These approaches view regional integration as a plurality of individual material interests ultimately converging to produce a single collective pursuing the same basic goals. However, what they ignore is that ideological and philosophical commitment to the integration process by the actors is needed in order to reinforce these material expectations (Haas 1972).

In an attempt to redress some of these limitations of theory, this study shall place as its central concern the role of ideology in the integration process. The major claim of this study is that the integration movement is weak and unstable because it is not based upon nor guided by an ideology of regionalism. This claim will be the main hypothesis of this study. Support for this claim is found in chapters 3, 4 and, particularly, chapter 5, where a survey of elite attitudes toward integration indicates that what exists among the elite of Saint Lucia and Jamaica is a set of diffused regionalist sentiments instead of an ideology of regionalism. This sentiment appears to be stronger among the Saint Lucian elite.

In order to place the remainder of this discussion in proper perspective, some important characteristics of Caribbean society will be outlined. In the first place, there is the need to understand the rationale for regional integration.

An Overview of Caribbean Society

Caribbean society has been shaped by colonialism. Not only did it fashion the institutions and define the social mores of the societies of the region, but it also resulted in the insular development of the territories. Each individual territory was more closely integrated with Britain, and later the United States of America than with its neighbours in the region. As Gordon Lewis succinctly puts it:

> the sweep of historical forces since the discovery has shaped the archipelago — colonization, slavery, the plantation system, sugar, Emancipation has shaped the West Indian society. The particular impact has naturally been different in each island society, since the region's anomalous decentralization has worked to isolate island from island, island-group from island-group. That explains still, the absence of any real pan-Caribbean consciousness and the continuing balkanization of the area (Lewis 1968:4).

The earliest period of British hegemony in the region was characterized by mercantilism, when the region was used primarily for the production of sugar. However, the industrial revolution ushered in a new era which saw direct foreign investment into the colonies, further entrenching them in the world economy as primary producers and targets for the export of imperialist capital. During the first half of the twentieth century British dominance in the region was supplanted by that of the United States, as the period of monopoly capitalism swept the modern world. This was the dawning of what came to be known as neo-colonialism, a time when the tentacles of American capitalism reached across the Third World through transnational corporations (TNCs) (Beckford and Witter 1985).

But the interest of the United States in the region was not simply restricted to the economic arena. United States expansionism in the region was evident since the eighteenth century after the American Civil War. It was predicated on a doctrine of "Manifest Destiny" which purported that it was a "law of nature" for people to expand or die. Correspondingly, the notion of "natural right", that expansion was legitimate because of concern with national security, was also a prevailing rationale for United States domination (G. Lewis 1968). Such views lay at the root of the Monroe

3

Doctrine and of United States foreign policy in the region. Nowadays, United States hegemony in the region is reflected in economic relations, the mass media, migration and the values of the people.

But the relations between the countries of the region and the two metropoles have not been totally one-sided. According to Brathwaite (1974), colonialism threw up a social system in the colonies in which those at the highest echelons of society maintained strong links with the hegemonic power. This link was also made with the United States as it assumed the role as the new hegemonic power. These links with the metropole were not simply the result of ethnic and cultural identification but were perhaps even more fundamentally a reflection of a situation in which those who controlled the means of production in the territories saw their interests as being closely tied to those of the metropole (Brathwaite 1974).

The implication of the foregoing is that Caribbean society evolved with a stronger identification with countries outside of the region than with those inside, notwithstanding intra-regional relations developed through migration and political unions.

The initial insertion of the region into the world economy as primary producers and later as transnational corporation (TNC) enclaves has resulted in the structural dependence of the regional economies. This view is supported by the New World Group who, during the 1960s, launched a scathing attack on Lewis's "industrialization by invitation" strategy of economic development (Girvan and Jefferson 1977). It is, however, worthy of note that the "Lewis strategy" and the critiques of it were all responses to the problem of development within the region. The small size of the regional economies, it was thought, constituted an inhibiting factor to industrial development. This perspective was widely articulated by writers such as William Demas who, in *The Economics of Development in Small Countries*, argued that "natural" variables, that is, natural resources and a critical mass of people, were the main determinants of a country's ability to industrialize (Payne 1980).

Demas was, in fact, following a long tradition of thought which informed British attempts at integration in the countries of the region. The West Indies Federation was established in large part to overcome the obstacles to development which were seen to be the result of small size (Springer 1962). This was also the underlying motive for the formation of CARIFTA and CARICOM. Achieving economic development has therefore been associated with regional integration in the Caribbean.

But, such an attempt at the formation of an integrated region has not been peculiar to the Caribbean. In fact, the Caribbean represents only a microcosm of what has been occurring in the wider world, particularly among Third World countries, and what had already become a feature of the developed world.

Regional Integration and Development

The earliest examples of two states uniting by free decision was the union between England and Scotland. This represented the first attempt at the creation of a federation without coercion. The United States of America was the first country of the modern era to have a federal constitution. That constitution was written by Anglo-Americans. The idea of regional integration without force is therefore rooted, fundamentally, in the Anglo-Saxon tradition. Switzerland and Germany are the only real examples of federations outside the Anglo-Saxon world. Not surprisingly, they modelled their structures on the American system (Spinelli 1974).

Since the Second World War there has been a shift to more pragmatic forms of regional integration, with greatest emphasis on economic integration — the earliest and perhaps most notable example being the European Economic Community (EEC) which was formed during the 1950s. Although a response to the decline in European economies and perceived Soviet threat, it was, more importantly, an expression of a thriving supranational ideology which had taken hold in Western Europe after the nationalist conflicts of the Second World War (Hodges 1972). The EEC, therefore, emerged against a background of an ideology which eschewed narrow nationalism and supported regionalism not simply as a means to an end, but as an end in itself.

The rationale for regional integration relates to augmenting security arrangements and facilitating economic development through trade creation and trade diversion provided by a larger market. In the Third World, regional integration has as its primary concern economic development and economic growth. Axline (1979:9) notes as an argument for integration in the Third World that "economic development is to be achieved by industrialization which in turn is to be advanced through regional integration".

Small wonder that a plethora of integration movements emerged between the sixties and seventies. In Latin America, the Latin American Free Trade Association (LAFTA) was inaugurated in 1962. LAFTA, which later was to become the Latin American Integration Movement (ALADI), was concerned with economic and functional co-operation in areas of mutual interest. Out of LAFTA emerged a sub-group known as the Andean Pact which comprised five Latin American countries. The intention of this group was to deepen integration among themselves and increase their bargaining power in LAFTA as so-called Lesser Developed Countries (LDCs). The other integration movement which emerged in Latin America was the Central American Common Market (CACM) made up of Central American countries intent on co-operating in areas of economic interest.

In Asia the Association of South-East Asian Nations (ASEAN) was established in 1967 in an effort to accelerate economic development among its constituent countries. In the Pacific, the South Pacific Bureau for Economic Co-operation was set up in 1973 to improve co-operation and trade and economic matters among its members. In Africa a number of integration movements took root. In 1963 the Organization of African Unity (OAU) was founded to assist with the anti-colonial struggles and promote economic development through trade among all but two African countries. In 1964 the Customs and Economic Union of Central Africa, and in 1976 the Economic Community of West African States were formed. In both cases, the primary concern was that of trade and economic co-operation. One of Africa's most recent integration movements is the Southern African Development Co-ordination Conference (SADCC). This movement, comprising the frontline states, was founded in 1979. It is concerned with reducing dependence on South Africa and co-ordinating foreign policy towards the liberation of South Africa and Namibia — (the latter having subsequently gained its independence).

Over the years, the viability of these integration movements has been challenged by the vicissitudes of the world economy. For example, intra-regional trade of the developing countries as a percentage of their exports as a whole dropped from some 28 per cent in the first half of 1981 to under 25 per cent in the first half of 1982 (McIntyre 1984). CARICOM in particular has not fared well in such circumstances. In fact, McIntyre has noted that CARICOM is among the group of integration movements in the Third World which has made limited progress with the expansion of intra-regional trade. Between 1980 and 1987 CARICOM trade has averaged only 8 per cent of the total trade of member states comprising the movement. With the exception of some parts of Africa, this figure ranks lower than that for ALADI, 14 per cent; CACM, 22 per cent; and ASEAN, 50 per cent. In addition, intra-regional trade in CARICOM as a percentage of exports is one of the smallest compared to all developing countries. The 1980 figures of intra-regional trade as a percentage of exports show CARICOM, 32 per cent; ALADI, 48 per cent; CACM, 71 per cent; and ASEAN, 50 per cent (McIntyre 1984).

Compared with the EEC, the performance of CARICOM as a regional grouping is even more disappointing. Since its inauguration in 1957 and over the period to 1986, trade within the EEC has increased sixteen-fold *(Europe in Figures* 1988). At present, intra-regional trade accounts for more than 50 per cent of total external trade of member countries. The Community anticipates that with the creation of large internal markets in 1992 an impetus will be added to intra-community trade whose share to total trade went up from 35 per cent in 1956 to 58 per cent in 1986.

One important factor which has facilitated these strides in economic integration is the fact that the EEC has succeeded in creating a customs union with a common customs tariff and has been able to eliminate customs barriers between member states. The Community has taken even greater steps towards achieving a more integrated and united Europe through the Single European Act. The Act, signed in February 1986 came into force on 1 July 1987 and is designed to increase co-operation among member countries in economic, social and political spheres. Among other things, the Act includes freedom of movement of people and goods; more equitable distribution of wealth among member countries; and greater control over the monetary system. In all of these ways and more the powers of the Community have been extended to give greater control over policy making at the national level.

In the case of CARICOM, its problems have not been restricted to the economic sphere, although that remains the primary preoccupation of the movement. CARICOM has, since its inauguration, encountered tremendous obstacles to the realization of a truly integrated region, as is demonstrated in chapter 4. For example, in the area of foreign policy co-ordination CARICOM has been unable to adopt a common position on a large number of important issues. The major reason for such difficulties, it must be reiterated, results from the claim that the movement is not based upon nor guided by an ideology of regionalism.

Method and Definitions

In order to test the hypothesis of this study, a survey of elite attitudes towards integration was conducted in the countries of Jamaica and Saint Lucia between January and June 1988.

The reason for embarking on a survey of elite attitudes is that attitudes reflect in a substantive way the character of people's ideologies. In addition, no cross-national study exists in this area so it was decided to use the survey method since it is one of the most effective social scientific tools for capturing and categorizing people's attitudes.

The term "elite" was first used in the seventeenth century to describe commodities of a particular quality. The term was later used to connote a concept which was applied to so-called superior social groups. Within the social sciences the term was first used by Vilfredo Pareto in opposition to the notion of social classes, this latter concept being characteristic of Marxist literature (Bottomore 1966). Since then, the concept has often been used throughout the social sciences. However, Marxist writers have tended to avoid incorporating this concept of elite into their analyses because of its bourgeois origins. Throughout the literature, therefore, there exist many arguments either in support of or against the use of the concepts of class and elite as appropriate categories for classifying different socio-economic groups. Lack of space does not allow for any serious treatment of this issue here. Suffice it to say, that the conflicting concepts of class and elite are not necessarily irreconcilable.

The term "elite" as used in this discussion refers to a group of people who are not necessarily part of the ruling class but who possess the ability to seriously influence the social process. More specifically, elites are groups of people, normally professionals, who occupy top private or public organizational positions which allow them to make or influence policy at national and/or regional level. Their ability to impact on policy may be of a bureaucratic nature or through public opinion.

The elite is not a homogeneous group. There are a number of elite groups which have varying degrees of influence on society. Elite groups also possess the capacity to effect fundamental changes within the social structure. For example, it was a political elite which was in the forefront of the Grenada Revolution of 1979 (Searle 1983). On the other hand, elite groups may be forced out of spheres of influence because of ruling class pressure. The People's National Party during the 1980 elections is a case in point (Stephens and Stephens 1986). The ability of elite groups to effect social change is a function of (i) their relationship to the means of reproduction — social, political and economic institutions; (ii) the hegemonic strength of the ruling class; (iii) the objective socio-economic and political conditions which characterize the society.

One can therefore construct three basic elite categories — cultural, political and economic. These elite types are by no means immutable, exclusive or exhaustive. They are based on the major institutions of re-production which are normally imperative for the longevity of any social formation.

The cultural elite is concerned primarily with the reproduction of ideas. This task inevitably involves the interaction with mass culture which may be, at some time, antagonistic to ruling class ideas.

The political elite is normally the guardian of the state in the interest of the ruling class. The role of this group is concerned with ensuring the preservation of law and order and the protection of ruling class property. It is quite possible, however, for this section to develop an identity of its own and even subvert ruling class interests. Witness, for example, Guyana under Burnham, where the state became the biggest property owner and developed a bureaucratic bourgeoisie under the guise of co-operative socialism (Thomas 1984).

The economic elite has as its main task the management of conflict between capital and labour in the interest of the ruling class (or the state). Because of this intimate relationship with the ruling class, this group is forced to acquiesce and collaborate with the ruling class.

An understanding of elite attitudes toward integration is therefore central to the comprehension of the ideological forces upon which policies at the regional level are based and directed, since it is the elite which is engaged in the day-to-day management of Caribbean society.

The survey of elite attitudes included a total of 182 interviews, 100 conducted in Jamaica and 82 in Saint Lucia. The countries were chosen for: (i) their geographical location, Saint Lucia lying in the centre of the Eastern Caribbean archipelago while Jamaica is the most westerly of the territories; (ii) the different levels of development, Saint Lucia being an LDC and Jamaica a More Developed Country (MDC) — features allowing for sample representations from which many of the inferences from the data can be applied across the rest of the region; (iii) easy access to respondents and the availability of technical assistance, such as libraries, computers and qualified manpower.

Each sample is divided into three elite groups: cultural, political and economic. Since these groups are not exclusive, in cases where a respondent fits into multiple categories, what is perceived to be the respondent's most dominant activity determines the choice of elite category.

The cultural elite are those people who occupy positions which enable them to influence public opinion significantly and to shape people's ideas about society. This group comprises persons operating in cultural and sporting organizations (cultural activists), the media, educational institutions and religious organizations.

The economic elite are those who either own companies or occupy positions of influence in public or private business. Such a group includes managers of private or public statutory corporations, board directors, and senior civil servants in managerial positions.

The political elite is classified as those who occupy positions which enable them to make or directly influence political decisions. This group includes politicians, civil servants who formulate political policy, and trade union leaders. Tables 1.1 and 1.2 give a breakdown of the two samples according to group classification.

Table 1.1: Type of Elite by Number Interviewed
(Jamaica)

Type of elite	Number
Political	
Civil servants	10
Politicians	17
Trade unionists	3
Cultural	
Cultural activists	11
Religious leaders	3
Journalists/Commentators	7
Teachers/University lecturers	11
Economic	
Managers (public)	8
Managers (private)	27
Civil servants	3
Total	100

The survey is based on reputational sampling. The selection of the sample was done from a "master" list drawn up with the assistance of a number of government and private agencies in the two countries. In Jamaica, a list of top business persons was obtained from the Private Sector Organization of Jamaica and the Jamaica Manufacturers Association. A list of top party and trade union officials and representatives of the Jamaica Labour Party (JLP), and the People's National Party (PNP) was compiled with the assistance of some of the respective party officials. In addition, a

Table 1.2: Type of Elite by Number Interviewed
(Saint Lucia)

Type of elite	Number
Political	
Civil servants	11
Politicians	6
Trade unionists	5
Cultural	
Cultural activists	7
Religious leaders	3
Journalists/Commentators	8
Teachers/University lecturers	12
Economic	
Managers (public)	6
Managers (private)	16
Civil servants	7
Unclassified	1
Total	82

list of major religious organizations, media houses, educational and cultural institutions was used to obtain the names of a number of people in prominent positions.

In Saint Lucia, a similar approach was adopted. Information on leading business persons was obtained from the OECS Secretariat while a list of party officials from the Saint Lucian Labour Party (SLP), the United Workers Party (UWP) and the Progressive Labour Party (PLP) was compiled with the assistance of party officials. A list of media houses, educational and cultural institutions and trade unions was the source for names of the major actors. During the course of the survey, names of members of elite groups were added or deleted as a result of suggestions made by various respondents regarding people's positions and influence in the society.

Ideally, it would have been much better to survey both elite and mass attitudes in more than two countries in order to get a more comprehensive picture of regional attitudes. However, limited financial resources, shortage of manpower and insufficient time rendered an elite survey in only two countries the most feasible. Thus, while the results are generalized for the region, this is done with the recognition that different attitudes may well exist in the territories not surveyed. Hopefully, future research will provide a more comprehensive survey and analysis of the ideological tendencies which characterize the region.

In discussing the major claim of this study, the remainder of this discussion is structured along the following lines. Chapter 2 engages in a brief review of the literature and suggests an alternative framework for approaching the study of Caribbean regional integration.

Chapter 3 examines the evolution of regional integration in the Caribbean in order to place the movement in some conceptual framework. Focus is placed on the development of federalism through to CARICOM, in order to see the evolutionary forces involved.

Chapter 4 seeks to show that CARICOM is weak and unstable. This is done with respect to the Treaty, policies in relation to functional co-operation and the Common Market. The lack of an ideology of regionalism is advanced as a major explanation for the state of the movement.

Chapter 5 is concerned with the analysis of the data on elite attitudes. The inferences drawn from the data support the main hypothesis, that the integration movement is not based upon nor guided by an ideology of regionalism.

Finally, the conclusion (chapter 6) summarizes the overall findings of the study, pointing to areas in which steps can be taken to develop an ideology of regionalism.

CHAPTER 2

Towards an Alternative Framework for the Study of Regional Integration

In this chapter an attempt is made to review some of the literature on Caribbean regional integration with a view to suggesting an alternative approach to the study of integration within the region.

Approaches to the Study of Regional Integration

Much of the theorizing on regional integration has arisen out of European experiences. Hansen (1972) notes that for some time now Europe has remained the focal point for the majority of works on integration. However, within recent times there has been an attempt to apply integration theory to Third World countries. An insight into integration theory is therefore of prime importance if one is to contextualize the whole gamut of writings which seeks to analyse Caribbean regional integration.

An important caveat in reviewing these approaches is to recognize that integration theory is still very much at the developing stages. Hence, to call these approaches theory may lead to the perpetuation of a misnomer (Hodges 1972). This becomes obvious if one agrees with the view that the concern of theory is to describe the process which it seeks to deal with, isolate the various stages which characterize the process, explain the reasons for these stages and predict what is likely to happen, given certain conditions. Integration approaches undoubtedly do not fulfill all of these requirements.

There are basically three main approaches to the study of integration. They are the federalist, the transactionalist, and the neo-functionalist.

The federalist approach is concerned with the creation of supranational institutions to ensure efficiency, and the decentralization of bodies to bring about political democracy. According to its exponents, the success of integration is premised on the need to attain political consensus even in the face of adverse social and economic conflict. A political solution is seen as the answer to uniting diverse social and economic interests which may characterize a region. This approach depends on a highly developed legal system. The central assumption of federation is the primacy of politics. That is to say, the success of federation is the function of the ability to reach a consensus out of political will. The federalist approach is not seen in the literature as a theoretical one. As Hodges puts it, it is "... more a strategy for fullfulling a common purpose and common needs than a theory explaining how these integration forces arise" (Hodges 1972:13).

One of the greatest dangers of using this approach is that implicitly it assumes that a federal structure is workable wherever and at whatever level it operates. That is to say, federal structures can be applied effectively in any region, whether it be among developed or developing countries. The wholesale imposition of this model on post-colonial societies runs the risk of failure because of these countries' peculiar historical development. Most post-colonial societies were more economically and politically integrated with the mother country than with countries within their common geographical area. This inevitably meant that a closer identity would have been developed with the mother country. To compound the situation, these states did not often develop efficient political structures and institutions which could have been easily adapted to supranational bodies.

Unlike federalism which places greatest emphasis on the legal institutional framework, the transactionalists are preoccupied with the development of a sense of community. This community identity is supported by a common value system. The approach emphasizes the role of communication in the creation and reproduction of community. Karl Deutsch, one of the major exponents of this approach, argues that integration is the condition in which people of a particular region have a sense of community (Deutsch 1972). In other words, co-operation is reached through consensus and is facilitated by a number of institutions concerned with policy implementation.

Following Deutsch, transactionalists identify two types of communities. The first is the Amalgamate Security Community formed by a merger of two or more previously independent countries into a single body under some form of government. The second is the Pluralistic Security Community where separate governments retain legal independence but also institutionalize some forms of co-operation. The success of these two forms of integration depends on the existence of a strong sense of community.

The transactionalists see transactions between member countries as a prerequisite for a successful community. Hence, in order to determine the degree of interdependence prevailing within a particular region, an attempt is made to measure the level of transactions. According to its exponents, if an individual is satisfied with the outcome of a transaction he is more likely to repeat the process. But transactions in themselves are not sufficient. It is quite possible to have transactions but a poor communication system which emphasizes divergent values and expectations to the detriment of the community. In general, successful integration results only if the ability of the system to respond to demands is equal to or better than the level of demands.

There have been a number of criticisms of this approach. First, while transaction flows may be an indication of interactions within the integration process, transactions do not cause integration but are, fundamentally, a reflection of the process. Predicting the course of integration becomes problematic if one uses trends in transaction flows as the unit of analysis.

Secondly, the approach is unable to estimate unquantifiable transactions such as attitudes and values, both of which, according to the approach, are central to the integration process.

This leads to a third weakness, namely, although there is recognition of the importance of values in promoting a sense of community, the analysis stops short of showing the ideological underpinnings of such values and how they impact on integration.

Neo-functionalist analysis grew out of the functionalist approach to integration. The greatest output of functionalist literature occurred during the period between the two world wars (Deutsch 1972). In this approach, the most important preoccupation was the creation of international organizations to perform welfare tasks. The ultimate intention of this school was the elimination of the nation state, which was perceived as constituting the most serious threat to world peace. The approach has also supported the view that the nation state was unable to perform many of the tasks needed for development, such as air transport and disease control, among others. The intention of the school was to encourage governments to entrust the performance of these tasks to so-called non-political technical experts, all of whom would operate within an international organization. The effective completion of these tasks would lead to further co-operation in other areas by the actors. However, neo-functionalists were dissatisfied with the lack of clarity and specificity of the functionalists. In addition, they questioned the idea of universal welfare needs which suggests a congruence of values across nations (Hodges 1972).

The neo-functionalists, in contrast to the transactionalists, emphasize the pluralist nature of modern society. Such societies, in their estimation, are comprised of a number of competing elites and interest groups. Ernest Haas, the leading architect of this school, defines integration as: "The process whereby political actors in several distinct national settings are persuaded to shift their loyalties, expectations and political activities towards a new and larger centre, whose institutions possess or demand jurisdiction over pre-existing national states" (Haas 1972:20).

Implicit in the definition is the attempt to escape the assumption made by the transactionalists that consensus exists among the actors of the integration movement. By avoiding this assumption, neo-functionalists are able to distinguish between the situation prior to integration and after the process has commenced.

Neo-functionalists believe that people of different countries co-operate because of pragmatic interests. They concentrate on the collective decision making process and ways in which politically significant elites move away from national towards supranational oriented policy making. There is also the attempt to monitor the changes of values among these significant groups from national to regional orientation. Haas sees the gradual "politicisation" of technical aspects of the development process among the actors involved as an ultimate outcome. He further states that this "politicisation" process succeeds and, as "the national actors perceive that their interests are best served by delegation of national decision powers to the new supranational body in one field, it is likely that they will apply the lesson to integration elements in other fields" (Haas 1972:23).

Like the approach of the transactionalists and the federalists, neo-functionalism has also had its share of criticism. The first one is identified by Hoffmann (1966) who argues that within the European context neo-functionalism does not pay attention to the impact of the international political and economic environment on national and regional policies. By ignoring this factor, neo-functionalists analyse only part of a reality which has increasingly become one of great interdependence.

Secondly, by emphasizing elite actions, neo-functionalism, as Wiltshire-Brodber (1984) states, has led analysts to ignore integration at the mass level thereby capturing only part of the integration process.

The third criticism comes from Haas himself who argues that the emphasis on pragmatism for economic gains has inherent limitations. Haas (1972:25) recognizes that "without a deep ideological or philosophical commitment to reinforce these material expectations, there is no inherent pressure for further integrative attempts".

Although each of these approaches has at some time or the other influenced works on Caribbean integration, federalism and, to a much greater extent, neo-functionalism have been by far the most influential. This is true if one examines the writings on the West Indies Federation and CARICOM. Both CARIFTA and CARICOM have been greatly influenced by neo-classical economic theory which, incidentally, is the bedrock of neo-functionalist analysis. Admittedly, as shall be seen later, some of these writings have attempted to overcome many of the limitations which are inherent in integration theorizing. For instance, attempts have been made to address the impact of the world economy, as well as the conflicting national interest, on the movement. Also, some amount of discussion (though far from enough) has sought to look at the role of class and other social groups within the integration process. There has also been concern with issues of culture and ideology and their role in the integration process. Nevertheless, so far there has been no published work which deals in detail with the role of ideology in regional integration.

Approaches to Caribbean Integration — A Review of the Literature

Most of the literature on Caribbean integration can be classified under four, though not exclusive, categories. They include economic, political, cultural and multidisciplinary approaches. These classifications are based on the emphases of the works and are useful not only because they allow for an isolation of the major tendencies, but also because they embrace practically the entire gamut of writings on integration in the region.

A sample of these writings, which clearly highlight the above approaches and which, for the most part, are among the more recognized and celebrated works, includes in the economic category a publication by a group of Caribbean experts appointed by the Common Market Council of Ministers to prepare a strategy for integration during the decade of the 1980s

(Ten Years of CARICOM 1984). The publication is concerned with the achievements and shortcomings of regional integration. It identifies problems such as failure to embark on areas of production integration and the inability of governments to effectively manage balance of payments crises as significant limitations of the movement. Among the suggestions made to improve integration are production integration, the development of monetary control systems, and the upgrading of administrative mechanisms. Unfortunately, the writers, true to the strict tradition of neo-functionalism, ignore the impact of social and political variables and treat integration as merely a technical issue.

Bennett (1984) explores a set of approaches to the administration of external payments by CARICOM countries, while simultaneously examining the short-run payments problem which results from policies of national interest. His analysis is restricted to an assessment of exchange rate policy, non-tariff barriers to trade, and initiatives in the area of regional payments arrangements. He shows that improved economic management and a co-ordinated regional approach to the administration of these payments are necessary if economic decline is to be overcome. Unfortunately, his analysis stops there for he ignores the impact of the world economy on the administration of payments. Additionally, because of his narrow economic focus, he is unable to incorporate political and sociological factors which partly determine the nature of economic policy adopted by governments. Witness, for example, Jamaica under Manley in the seventies and Bishop in Grenada during the revolution adopting unorthodox economic policies in response to ideological persuasion.

Trevor Farrell (1983) sees the problem of balance of payments as part of a wider problem of economic development. Farrell is of the view that political unification is necessary for the success of a development strategy where one section of the economy is export oriented and the other regionally oriented. For Farrell, balance of payments problems and conflicts within the regional movement reflect the inability of governments to adopt this strategy of development. The problem with Farrell's analysis is that he incorrectly assumes that there exists a convergence of interests as regards economic development within CARICOM. Although he recognizes the importance of values in economic development, there is no mention of them in connection with political unification. He therefore ignores the importance of a cohesive set of ideas in motivating and sustaining a movement with diverse interests.

It is probably true to state that, of all integration theorists, Demas, undoubtedly, has had the most influence on the concept and structure of the regional integration movement. Like Farrell, he has consistently advocated political unification as the most effective form of integration. Demas (1974) outlines a number of reasons for economic and political integration in the region. In addition, he examines some of the strengths and weaknesses of CARICOM. He identifies important advances made in the area of functional co-operation, the integration of production, and joint development of national resources, among others. The weaknesses relate to lack of local ownership and control of resources, failure to rationalize air transport and co-ordinate foreign policy and the lack of people involvement in CARICOM, to mention a few. Demas attributes these difficulties to the youthful nature of the movement (only one year old at the time), along with the need for political will among the regional leaders.

Demas (1987), thirteen years later, calls for the political unification of the OECS as a necessity and as an example to the wider region. In this publication, he sets out the pros of political unification and the cons of the continued fragmentation. Demas is insistent that in spite of the advances made by CARICOM, political unification is a prerequisite for its sustained viability in the future.

Demas (1976), in a book divided into fifteen essays, shows how economic integration may be achieved. In this work, also, there is some mention of the need for political unification similar to that advocated by Arthur Lewis (see W.A. Lewis 1950).

Although Demas's call for political unity remains unheeded by regional leaders, his proposals for economic integration have had a tremendous impact on the integration process. He outlines a strategy for economic integration which served as a blue print for CARIFTA and later CARICOM (Demas 1965). In this publication, he outlines a number of structural deficiencies of the regional economies which, in his view, can only be overcome with regional economic integration. He further argues that most of these deficiencies are difficult to overcome because of the small size of the countries. Using a modified form of neo-classical trade theory, Demas suggests a strategy of collective import substitution to be facilitated through regional integration.

There are two serious contradictions which run through Demas's works. The first conundrum in which he finds himself is that on the one hand, he advocates political unity, which requires a convergence of ideas and an ideology of regionalism, while on the other hand, he supports neo-functionalist integration which heralds economic pragmatism and plurality of interest.

Secondly, Demas argues that the obstacle to political unity is the lack of political will among the leaders in the region. Yet he is adamant that there is a West Indian identity and that there is a likeness of thought and ideology as regards regionalism. Is Demas separating the notion of political will from ideology and identity? Ideology motivates political action, while the strength of identity partly determines the regionalist character of such action. Hence, to separate ideology and identity from political will is totally erroneous. Demas seems to be starting with the presumption that there already exist ideological forces within the region which facilitate regional integration. He clearly articulates the view that one of the cases for political integration is the need to consolidate the West Indian identity (Demas 1987). Is this the reason for Demas's inability to pay sufficient attention to the issue of ideology in regionalism? Or does it reflect a misunderstanding of its role in the integration process? Whichever of these observations is correct it is the case that the regional movement, which has followed closely many of the tenets proposed by Demas, has also suffered because of a lack of attention by policy makers to the critical role of ideology in the development of regionalism.

A number of writers have advanced the view that the political and economic policies adopted by regional governments have been detrimental to the integration movement. Eckstein (1978), Hippolyte-Manigat (1979), Bernal et al. (1984) and Hall and Blake (1976) have all argued that the conflict between national and regional policies has resulted in a crisis within CARICOM.

In his paper, Eckstein argues that there is no economic integration to speak of in the region. He states that the idea of free trade is a myth since member countries have continued to engage in blatant trade protectionism and insular economic policies. He also argues that the MDCs are the greatest beneficiaries of intra-regional trade, thereby encouraging unequal development. Finally, excessive jingoism and ideological differences have in his view prevented the deepening of integration.

Hippolyte-Manigat endorses many of the points made by Eckstein. Her study, which is comparatively more comprehensive, focuses on trade relationships and political interaction between member territories from 1973 to 1979. She views the crisis within CARICOM at two levels. First, there is a crisis of national economic development and secondly, there is a crisis of regional development which grows out of, and is exacerbated by, the national crisis. The national crises within CARICOM are invariably products of, or are influenced by, a decline in the world capitalist economy. Trade conflicts and breached agreements are the result of the dependent nature of the regional economies along with insular development policies adopted by the member countries. Ideological conflicts have tended to intensify these tensions. Hippolyte-Manigat is therefore led to ask in her conclusion whether national or regional policy should take precedence. Her answer an unequivocal statement of support for regional over national policy making.

Bernal et al. while recognizing the national-regional dichotomy, do not place as much emphasis on it as Hippolyte-Manigat. The article is concerned more with Jamaica and the crisis within CARICOM. Its title is perhaps misleading since it seems to suggest that the crisis within CARICOM is somewhat unrelated to Jamaica. The paper argues that because of a downturn in the world economy during the 1970s, trade between Jamaica and its CARICOM partners declined in absolute terms. Political conflicts arising out of ideological differences have also precipitated conflicts within the movement. The writers further contend that the lack of consensus on a whole range of issues and a movement away from political unity within CARICOM have further weakened the movement. Their solution is for member countries to adjust national economic policies making them compatible with regional objectives.

Blake and Hall follow a similar line of argument. They pay closer attention to changes in political regimes and their impact on economic policies. They also note that the same external political factors, principally, the emergence of the Carter administration in the United States, had positive consequences for self-determination and integration. Theirs is more of a descriptive study and is not committed to offering solutions.

Overall, the four studies are very interesting and extremely informative. However, a major weakness of them all is that they are not grounded in social theory. Thus, with the exception of Hippolyte-Manigat, they tend to over-emphasize the technical side of the issues. Further, although the writers see the regional-national conflict as a fundamental weakness of the movement, there is no discussion of its historical development and how it may be resolved. There is little consideration for the role of class and other sectional interests and how these groups relate to the integration movement. Finally, although there is recognition that ideological conflicts have inhibited closer integration, concern with values, attitudes and ideology remains peripheral to the discussions.

Most of the literature in the political category is concerned with the impact of the global political economy on the integration process. V. Lewis (1983; 1984) and Villamil (1984) fall into this group. There is another school of analysts which tends to concentrate on the insular phenomena within the region. Axline (1979) and Payne (1980) represent two examples.

Lewis (1984) advances the argument that regional co-operation declined during the 1970s. The main reason for this was that the global economy was undergoing periods of instability resulting in national economic crises. The unilateral approach by CARICOM countries to countering these debilitating effects resulted in political conflicts across the region. Lewis (1983) is concerned with the inability of governments to learn from the problems brought on by the global economy in the seventies. He suggests that one way of overcoming regional disintegration is by strengthening CARICOM institutions.

Villamil argues along much the same lines as Lewis. He adopts a core-periphery approach, highlighting the problems caused by sectoral interests and TNC control within the regional movement. He concludes on a rather pessimistic note, suggesting that economic transformation remains a difficult task because of the geo-political nature of United States-Caribbean relations.

Both Lewis and Villamil have made important contributions to knowledge especially in relation to Caribbean integration within the international context. Nevertheless, both writers are perhaps guilty of too much emphasis on external variables as an explanation for the complex and historical problem of national conflicts within the regional movement. The non-recognition of other potential integrative elements leads Villamil to the conclusion that the region is unable to achieve autonomy and self-reliance, while Lewis argues for greater institutional integration without reference to the potential internal elements which could help to achieve such.

Axline is preoccupied with an analysis of the progress of integration through the prisms of a theoretical construct. His model sees integration as moving from Type 1 or *laissez-faire* movement to Type 2 movement distinguished by the establishment of a common external tariff; and finally to Type 3 movement characterized by a combination of Type 1 and Type 2. Opportunity cost is the foundation for the bargaining process among regional partners and accounts for movements through the stages. Axline places CARICOM at the Type 2 stage and argues that political will is the major determining factor for achieving Type 3 movement.

Payne, on the other hand, places more emphasis on an empiricist approach. His main argument is that the problem of integration results from an MDC-LDC split; insularity of the country; obstinacy of political leadership; and sectional interests of some of the regional actors.

Both writers have contributed considerably to a detailed understanding of the political and economic process within CARICOM. Nevertheless, Gittens (1983) in a rejoinder to both publications correctly argues that both of the analyses are static. Both writers have failed to locate the region adequately within the wider world economy and have insufficiently discussed the historical, social and economic forces which have determined the structure of the societies. In addition, there is, surprisingly, very little on the role of values, attitudes and ideologies, all of which help to determine political decision which Axline sees as central to deeper integration.

Works within the multidisciplinary framework include Thomas and Brewster (1967) and Thomas (1975; 1979). These works adopt a political economy approach. Thomas and Brewster did their work before the formation of CARIFTA and many of their suggestions for economic integration (for example, production integration) were incorporated into the CARIFTA and CARICOM treaties. The original concern was to suggest a strategy for regional economic integration based on import substitution. The publication emphasizes the need for a regional approach to industrial and agricultural development, utilizing as far as possible local resources and creating linkages between sectors; the need for the transformation of the national economy away from TNCs to local ownership; and the necessity for the adoption of relevant technology. There is also mention of the need for a change in cultural values away from dependence on the metropolitan countries to greater self-reliance. While there is no explicit discussion on the role of social classes, the implications are that this issue has to be tackled to ensure development of a mass integration movement.

The publication has two important shortcomings. First, not enough is said about the impact of the world economy on the ability to achieve integration. Secondly, and more importantly, coming after the demise of the Federation, Thomas and Brewster, astonishingly, say little or nothing about the political and ideological forces which impact on the ability of the region to become integrated. As a consequence, although the publication has made a number of critical points about the need for self-reliance and collective development, it falls down because of its inability to identify and seriously discuss the motivating ideological factors which could facilitate the adoption of the required policies. Thomas and Brewster failed to realize that without a favourable ideological climate their proposals could not be implemented successfully.

Thomas's works (1975, 1979) are written within a Marxian framework intent on advocating a new approach to integration. These works are critical of the way in which CARICOM operates, suggesting that like the Federation and CARIFTA, it only serves to perpetuate ruling class interests. In Thomas (1975) a Marxist theory of integration is outlined. The writer argues in favour of socializing the means of production, developing a mass movement in favour of integration and transforming the national economies. The purpose of integration would be to consolidate and heighten the struggle towards socialism.

Both of the works add a freshness to the debate, not only because of their analytical rigour but also because of the consideration given to social factors in integration. Marxist approach notwithstanding, Thomas pays inadequate attention to the role of the superstructure, as there is not enough discussion on the role of values and ideology in the integration process.

Other works which fall within the multidisciplinary framework but with a less radical approach are Williams (1965) and *Ten Years of CARICOM* (1984).

Williams is concerned with an examination of the reasons for the failure of the Federation and an assessment of efforts at regional economic integration. Written after the demise of the Federation and before the formation of a regional economic community, the publication is important if only because it illustrates some of the thinking which did then, and still continues to inform policy formulation within the regional integration movement.

The publication is essentially a collection of short essays in which Williams seeks to absolve himself for the failure of the Federation. Williams's overall thesis is that the efforts at federation and other forms of economic integration have failed because of interference from Britain and the United States of America and the insularity of regional leaders. He starts out by describing early attempts by foreign powers at creating an integrated region so as to ensure and maintain control over the region. He further argues that similar motives were behind British support for the Federation. The problem was, however, compounded by the fact that there was lack of consensus on the type of federal structure among the region's political leaders. Williams argues that only a strongly centralized federation could have worked in order to ensure full independence and cohesion within the movement.

Williams goes on to outline further attempts to create an economic community all of which were frustrated because of jingoism. His prognosis for the future of regionalism is pessimistic, to say the least, as he sees external dependency along with a lack of commitment to regionalism as fetters to regional unity.

Two important contributions of the work are: first, it documents the experiences of one of the leading figures of the integration movement thus capturing first-hand knowledge of some of the leading issues which afflicted early attempts at the Federation. Secondly, Williams's examination of the historical, sociological, political and economic factors with a view to exploring the shortcomings of efforts at regional integration enriches his analysis as he is able to integrate a number of important variables often overlooked by analysts whose approaches are uni-disciplinary.

There are two important weaknesses of the work. First, although Williams recognizes insularity and lack of cohesion as a major fetter to integration, he fails to examine the ideological factors which led to this situation. In addition, Williams does not even suggest what ideological factors are most likely to bring about successful regional integration. This leads to the second criticism which is that although Williams implicitly recognizes the lack of regionalist ideology as a problem, he advocates the formation of an economic union based on pragmatic and narrow economic interests. Nowhere in the publication is there a discussion of the role of values, norms or any aspect of the ideological mind-set necessary for the formation of an integrated region.

Ten Years of CARICOM is a fairly well balanced publication which contains a variety of articles with emphases in the areas of history, political science and economics. Most of the articles can easily fit into the four categories outlined earlier. Except for one article by Wiltshire-Brodber, all of them follow orthodox argumentation similar to most of those in the above discussion. Wiltshire-Brodber in "What Role do Caribbean People Play in Promoting Regional Integration: Toward a Wholistic Theory of Regional Integration" argues that cultural factors and migration have played decisive roles in the promotion of regional integration. She attempts to escape from the neo-classical institutional approach to integration with its uni-focal examination of economic variables, by concentrating on integration outside of the formal structures. Wiltshire-Brodber's contribution in this area is quite creative, enlightening and thought provoking. Nevertheless, her analysis might have benefited from ascribing greater significance to the role of culture as an important force within informal integration.

The writers within the cultural category examine issues of ideology and culture with reference to integration. Clarke (1984), Lowenthal (1984) and Thomas-Hope (1984) all argue that problems of identity and culture are important factors which inhibit proper regional integration. All three writers agree that the notion of a Caribbean identity, a prerequisite for integration, has not been developed. They see insularity resulting from the historical development of the region as an inhibiting factor to the creation of a strong regional identity. The lack of a regional consciousness is a fetter to regional unity. As Thomas-Hope puts it, "The failures of Caribbean integration are chiefly ascribed to the lack of a sense of identity" (1984:2).

However, while recognizing the important contribution these three writers have made to a greater understanding of non-material factors in regional integration, it is also true that the writings have been far from comprehensive in their analyses, and have given little consideration to economic variables. There seems to be a tendency to treat non-material factors as being autonomous. This clearly represents the other side of the coin where writers have also had a tendency to treat economic variables as if they too were autonomous and unrelated to non-material variables.

The result has been that the literature within the cultural category has tended to lose its explanatory effectiveness and attractiveness. This has been to the detriment of writings on Caribbean regional integration which, for the most part, have concentrated almost exclusively on the economic aspects of integration. The following section proposes an alternative theoretical framework for the analysis of Caribbean regional integration and represents an attempt to fill the gap by advocating a more comprehensive treatment of non-material variables.

Towards an Alternative Approach: The Role of Ideology in Regional Development

Much of the traditional social theorizing, particularly within the Marxist camp, maintains that within each socio-economic formation elements of the base and the superstructure constitute the main formative elements. These two constituents of social life are not detached and separate but are interrelated. The base refers to the totality of relations of production which is inherent to society. On the other hand, the superstructure constitutes an interrelated category of social phenomena, which includes such institutions as the state, the family structure, or the kinds of ideology prevalent in society (Eagleton 1983).

One social theorist who has paid great attention to the role of ideology in social development is Antonio Gramsci (Boggs 1976). Gramsci saw in the superstructure a certain degree of autonomy which was critical to how men conducted social life. He did not deny the primacy of the mode of production over the long run but he emphasized the reciprocity which existed between base and superstructure. He was therefore led to the conclusion that "it is these beliefs, attitudes and even superstitions and myths that are most 'material' or 'real' in their capacity to inspire people towards action" (Boggs 1976:37).

These elements of the superstructure constitute the ideology which partially determines people's behaviour. Gramsci, in fact, traced the lack of revolutionary zeal among the Italian working class to the internalization of a working class ideology. In other words, the everyday life of the mass of people was subordinated to the values, norms, attitudes, etc. of bourgeois society through its institutions of socialization. As a result, argues Gramsci, it encouraged a sense of passivity to political action against the ruling class thereby making the working class consent to their own exploitation (Boggs 1976). The importance of Gramsci's contribution, therefore, lies in his ability to show how social development is as much a response to economic forces as it is to ideology, each continually influencing the other.

Other social theorists have also demonstrated the role of ideology in social development. Max Weber, for example, in *The Protestant Ethic and the Spirit of Capitalism*, shows how protestantism as an ideology could have contributed to the development and reproduction of capitalism. The lifestyle associated with being a good protestant encouraged the cultivation of capitalist institutions. The idea of the "calling" encouraged entrepreneurship and frugality, both of which contributed to the accumulated process.

Marxists view the role of the superstructure as epiphenomenal, in direct opposition to Hegel who took an idealist position which saw material life as being determined by ideas. According to Marx:

> In direct contrast to the German philosophy which descends from heaven to earth, here we ascend from earth to heaven. That is to say, we do not set out from what men say, imagine, conceive, nor from men as narrated, thought of, imagined, conceived, in order to arrive at men in the flesh....Morality, religion, metaphysics, all the rest of ideology and their corresponding forms of consciousness thus no longer retain the semblance of independence....Life is not determined by consciousness, but consciousness by life (Tucker 1972: 118-19).

It is argued here that while Marx was correct to suggest that the base is not dictated by the superstructure and that both influence each other, it is questionable whether one can argue conclusively that the superstructure is merely epiphenomenal. Such an analytical method is simply one way of interpreting reality, a reality for which there can be no real distinction between either base or superstructure. In other words, to interpret an act as being determined by either base or superstructure runs one into posing the age-old adage "which came first — the chicken or the egg?" This issue is not one which can be supported by scientific proof but one which has to be determined on the basis of one's analytical preference. In other words, whether the economic system or ideology is proposed as the major determinant of change will be based first and foremost on how one constructs reality. Unlike the idealist or the materialist view of reality, it is being argued here that a theoretical construct which gives equal weight to both elements of what are called the base and superstructure is a more insightful analytical construct. The terms "base" and "superstructure" are replaced by the concepts "material structure" and "non-material structure." Such an approach recognizes that either element may dominate, depending on the particular circumstances. Hence, unlike classical Marxism, this approach does not assume that non-material aspects of social life, such as ideology, are epiphenomenal. This approach argues that effective change will most likely occur within society when emphasis is placed on both material and non-material elements of social life. However, emphasis placed on ideology will automatically affect the social, political and economic structures of society and vice versa. The survival of this ideology thus depends on the extent to which institutions are created to support it. Likewise, the institutions will only survive as long as there is an ideology which supports them.

The term "ideology" first used by the French philosopher Comte Antonio Detutt de Tracy (Gyorgy and Blackwood 1976) can be defined as:

... a set of ideas and beliefs through which we perceive the outside world and act upon our information. It is a medium through which we try to learn and comprehend the world, but it also generates emotions which hold people together. Finally, ideologies are action oriented. That is, they consist of ideas shared by many who act in unison or who are influenced to act in unison in order to accomplish posited ends (Macridis 1980:4).

Thus, factors which must be present for one to confirm the presence of an ideology include: (i) a shared coherent pattern of beliefs and ideas which hold people together both in times of prosperity and decline; (ii) the existence of a firm basis for formulating action and policies which invariably lead to the reproduction of the particular beliefs and ideas upon which those policies are based; (iii) a strong feeling among people that there are commonly held beliefs and ideas which are worth defending from both internal and external threat.

An ideology is thus different from ideation, which simply refers to the formation of ideas. An ideology leads to the development of a common world view among a group of people and is the motivating factor behind their actions to change reality. Such actions are normally done in unison as actors adopt a common position regarding what and how issues are to be tackled. Ideation does not necessarily lead to action, but is simply characterized by the formation of a diffused set of ideas which can ultimately lead to the formation of an ideology. Ideation is thus the process which precedes the formation of an ideology. It stands to reason that the reproduction of any social system must be dependent on an ideology which is successfully diffused and internalized by its constituents and on the requisite political, social and economic institutions to support this ideology being in place.

For the regional integration system to develop and sustain itself it must also be guided by an ideology which promotes regionalism. Institutions must be developed to shape an economic and political system which supports regionalism and which simultaneously diffuses integration ideas and values. The economic and political system will be influenced by, and in turn will influence attitudes and values. The successful diffusion of an ideology of regionalism will be reflected in relationships between the actors involved in the integration process. Policies at both national and regional level must of necessity be formulated within a regional context. For example, the co-ordination of economic and foreign policy measures of CARICOM member countries should be done in such a way as to promote the interests of the region as a whole over those of individual member countries. In other words, the motivating factor behind regional and national development must be the reproduction of regionalism itself. Put another way, an ideology of regionalism means that the goals of regional integration must be tied to achieving greater integration of the region.

An ideology of regionalism must, therefore, reflect a commonality of perception, explanation and action in relation to regional integration among the people of the region. Such an ideology could only be said to exist if the following are present: (i) a common perception of the region or a regional identity; (ii) a common set of explanations for the present state of the integration movement; (iii) a consensus on the need for and type of action required to strengthen and consolidate regionalism.

The absolute necessity for such an ideology becomes critical when one recognizes that the evolution of the region bequeathed a number of insular territories with strongest attachments to extra-regional countries. Rex Nettleford, for instance, has long argued that this situation constitutes a serious obstacle to regional integration (Nettleford 1978). As a result, he has advised that what is needed in the region is the cultivation of a sense of community which can best be promoted through cultural interaction. Accordingly, he has documented numerous instances where the arts have contributed to the development of regional identity. The development of a sense of identity, he argues, is a prerequisite for the achievement of economic or political integration without coercion. By implication, the development of a regional identity must precede the formation of an ideology of regionalism.

The concentration on technical and administrative aspects of integration has, as a consequence, led writers on Caribbean integration to de-emphasize the role of ideology as an necessary force in the integration process. Over the years, technocrats and analysts have concentrated on the construction of economic institutions with little consideration for values and attitudes. This action has in some instances affected people's attitudes towards a more regionalist outlook but has failed to lead to the creation of an ideology of regionalism. It seems that writers start off with either of the following two assumptions: (i) that the role of ideology is not very central to an analysis of integration, (ii) that an ideology of integration already exists within the region.

As the discussion has attempted to demonstrate, this approach is clearly inadequate. In fact, this inadequacy is further manifested in the following chapter which, in attempting to discuss the main claim of this study, not only examines technical and administrative issues but places central focus on the ideological context within which regional integration in the Caribbean emerged and has functioned over the years. By examining the evolution of regionalism, along with the knowledge of the early history of the region, one is able to account for the failure of the region to develop an ideology of regionalism.

CHAPTER 3

The Evolution of Regionalism in the Caribbean

The Early Development of the Federal Idea

Historically, regional integration in the Caribbean has always been seen as a means to an end and never as an end in its own right. Thus, a major weakness of the Federation and later attempts at economic integration was the conceptual framework which was not concerned with the reproduction of integration as a system but used it as a route to ensure political and economic viability within the wider world system. Hence, when the need for regional integration ceased to be central to the achievement of certain goals of individual territories, it was eschewed.

An additional but related factor is that, given the historical evolution of the region which developed as a number of insular units, it was imperative that for any strong integration system to survive there would be the need to develop a regional identity and an ideology to guide the integration process. Unfortunately, this was not done by the integrationists.

The idea of regional integration has existed in the Caribbean for a considerable period of time. Since the seventeenth century, attempts at uniting territories of the region to rationalize administrative costs of running the colonies occupied the thinking of the British Government. Such attempts, however, met with little success.

It had been the practice under colonialism for countries in the region to share governors. This was especially the case with the Leeward Islands, Jamaica, the Cayman Islands and Turks and Caicos. The Leeward Islands had a federation dating from 1871 which surrendered to the West Indies Federation of 1958. There was also an attempt during the 1870s to join Barbados in a federal union which included the Windward Islands. Such an attempt was however greeted with violent local opposition which ended in the Confederation Riots (Springer 1962). These riots brought to a temporary halt, until the West Indies Federation, British attempts at federation in the region.

But the idea of federation continued to be attractive to the British colonial civil servants who, on various occasions, made suggestions for federal schemes in articles or through speeches. In each case, the major concern was with the provision of more effective government and the rationalization of administration costs in the colonies.

The Royal Commission of 1882-1883, which was sent to enquire into ways of rationalizing economic administration in the Leeward and Windward Islands and Jamaica, recommended closer union, preferably of a federal type, as a solution. In 1894 a Royal Commission sent to Dominica to investigate conditions in the island suggested an administrative union of all the British Antilles under one governor general. The Royal Commission of 1896 and 1897 also suggested the unification of Barbados and the Windward Islands to make the management of these islands more efficient (Springer 1962).

However, the political agitation which began in the 1920s and the nationalist movement which consequently emerged added a new impetus to the federation idea. This movement of radical Caribbean leaders was led by Captain Andrew Cipriani (of Trinidad) and T.A. Marryshow (of Grenada) whose ideas and activities during the 1920s influenced leaders in other Eastern Caribbean countries (Mordecai 1963).

Cipriani, of upper middle class stock, founded the Workingmen's Association in 1919. This organization, which had a considerable lower class following, was concerned with issues such as land settlement, slum clearance, educational reform, and representation by elections to the legislature. Marryshow, a journalist of humble origins, formed the Representative Government Association of Grenada in 1914. He engaged in similar activities to Cipriani with the ultimate goal of achieving constitutional self-government. Marryshow and Cipriani became two of the earliest and foremost advocates of federation.

It should be noted that neither Cipriani nor Marryshow started out with the idea of federation. As Mordecai quite rightly argues, federation came into the picture because of the commonly held view that it was only through a collective approach that constitutional reforms and self-government could be achieved in the region. This resulted from the view that the individual colonies were too small to be viable entities. Thus, from the outset, federation represented a means to an end, to achieve self-government.

Early support for a federation came from various interest groups in the territories. These groups included the Barbados Chamber of Commerce and the Trinidad Chamber of Commerce, joined by the Jamaica Imperial Association and the Associated West Indian Chambers by the 1920s. These groups supported federation on the basis of the economic efficiency afforded by the amalgamation of the government administrations. As a result, in 1922 Major E.F. Wood (later Lord Halifax) went on a three-month tour of the region to see if conditions allowed for federation. The Wood Report, which was the result of the visit, concluded that public opinion did not support a federation of the region. Another outcome of the Wood visit was a decision to allow for constitutional changes around 1924, resulting in elected membership to some of the legislatures of the region. Voting was, however, restricted to exclude the working classes. The result of this situation was the growth of frustrated political leaders in the legislatures in both Trinidad and the Windward Islands, continuously clamouring for political change and the greater autonomy of the region (Mordecai 1963).

In spite of the Wood Report, the Colonial Office continued to show interest in the closer union of the territories. In 1926, the Secretary of State organized a conference of legislative nominees which proposed a Standing Conference to promote cooperation in a number of areas. The Conference was to act simply in an advisory capacity. In the opinion of the political leaders of the region, the Conference only served to divert attention from the immediate concern of federation. By 1931 the Conference had ceased to exist because of the lack of local interest. Nevertheless, during this period a number of conferences were held dealing with ways to improve economic cooperation at the regional level.

The Great Depression of the 1930s gave some impetus to the development of the idea of federation. In the Caribbean, sugar prices had been falling dramatically and wages were slashed while unemployment increased. The result of this situation was a number of riots across the region, beginning in Saint Christopher/Nevis in 1935 (Mordecai 1963). In view of the impending turbulence, the Colonial Office sent out a Sugar Commission to investigate the sugar industry. Apart from suggesting a need for the increased preference of colonial sugar to the United Kingdom market, the commissioners recommended an association of the Windward and Leeward Islands as a means of rationalizing the cost of government administration (Mordecai 1963).

As the economic and social crisis deepened and concern over the cost of political administration increased, both among the Colonial Office and the planters and merchants, it was announced in 1932 that a new commission, the Closer Union Commission, would be sent to the West Indies to examine the possibility of a closer union of the territories. Some political leaders within the region saw this as an opportunity to lobby their case for federation. In October 1932, at the invitation of the Dominica Taxpayers Reform Association, Caribbean leaders representing the Windward and Leeward Islands, along with Barbados and Trinidad, proceeded to draft a federal constitution along with a number of other proposals for the formation of a federation. Such proposals were subsequently rejected by the Closer Union Commission on the grounds that public opinion was against federation. The commission, however, proposed that the Windward and Leeward Islands be brought together under one governor (Springer 1963). It should be noted that during the Roseau Conference participants were divided over whether full dominion status should accompany the federation or should come afterwards. Although a compromise was struck at the time, this issue continued to be a source of controversy to the very end of the federation.

The disturbances of the 1930s also brought about serious changes in the political power structure of the colonies which, in turn, had serious implications for the formation of the federation. Out of the labour disturbances emerged staunch Caribbean nationalists such as Grantley Adams of Barbados, Norman Manley of Jamaica, Albertine Gomes of Trinidad, Hubert Critchlow of Guyana, among others, committed to the achievement of self-government. For them federation represented a means to self-government. By 1938, the political leaders of the Eastern Caribbean territories were unequivocally committed to federation.

In 1940 the Moyne Commission was sent to the colonies to look into the labour disturbances. Although admitting that sentiment among the leadership of the Eastern Caribbean was in favour of federation, it nevertheless suggested a federation of the Windward and Leeward Islands as a first step to full federation of the entire region. Mordecai argues that the main reason for this was because the Colonial Office preferred to have Jamaica included in its ideal federation (Mordecai 1963).

In 1945, Secretary of State Oliver Stanley sent a dispatch inviting the territories to meet and discuss the formation of a federation. The Caribbean Labour Congress (CLC) responded by bringing together most of the prominent labour leaders from the Caribbean. While the People's National Party, led by Norman Manley, was represented, the Jamaica Labour Party, led by Bustamante, who was chief minister at the time, was absent. Again, the issue of whether there should be full dominion status accompanying or after the federation resulted in a divided conference (Mordecai 1963). However, the final outcome called for a strongly centralized federation to be accompanied by full dominion status of the constituent countries.

In 1947 another despatch was sent by the new secretary of state, Creech-Jones, inviting leaders to a meeting in Montego Bay to further discuss the formation of a federation. At this conference the CLC presented their proposals arrived at during their earlier meeting. The proposals were ultimately rejected by the conference. The fiercest objections came from Bustamante, who argued that the idea of full dominion status accompanying the federation was nonsense since the countries were too poor to be totally viable even in a federal union. Out of the conference arose the Standing Closer Association Committee (SCAC), which was responsible for drafting the federal constitution. Federation, it therefore seemed, would act as a type of tutelage for self-government. The constitution would be drafted so as to allow each country to achieve its own constitutional advance. Nevertheless, because there was lack of consensus over the strength of the federal government and the status that should accompany the federated colonies, even after the drafting of the constitution, no final decision was taken on the type of federal structure.

In 1953 agreement for the commencement of the federation was secured at a conference held in London between Colonial Office officials and Caribbean leaders. This was followed by another London conference in 1956 at which a decision was made to start the federation on 23 February of that year. The federation was not inaugurated until 3 January 1958. It therefore proceeded without any final decision on the nature of the federal structure. As Mordecai puts it:

> What was decided in 1956 was to make a start with a federal structure which was really confederal rather than federal, postponing the problems of federal power for at least five years, in the hope that the passage of time, and experience of working together would make these problems easier to solve. But this decision did not stick ... all the problems were raised within the first year of the Federation's life; it was never allowed to cement (Mordecai 1963:61).

In 1962, the Federation came to an end as a result of the secession of Jamaica and, later, Trinidad. Attempts at a federation within the Eastern Caribbean all came to nought. The question which was to later haunt the analysts was: Why did the Federation fail? To such a perplexing question there has been no shortage of answers.

Millette (1969) argues that there have been three main approaches to the explanation of the failure of the Federation. First, there is the sociological explanation advanced by writers such as Etzioni (1965) and Bobb (1966). Secondly, there is the constitutional explanation advanced, for example, by

Proctor (1964). Finally, there is the personality explanation offered by writers such as W.A. Lewis (1965), Mordecai (1963) and Springer (1962). Although Springer and Mordecai stress the personality factor, they, unlike Lewis, also pay some attention to sociological and constitutional factors.

Of these three approaches the constitutional explanation appears to be the least attractive since, as Thomas argues, such an analysis may lead "... to a study of form and not content. The relevance of the legal document must lie in the way it affects the integration ... the legal document ... should not be mistaken for reality itself" (Thomas 1979: 286). For such a reason the sociological and personality explanations seem most productive here.

Both Mordecai and Lewis point to a conflict of interest between the leaders, namely Manley, Williams and Adams, as the fundamental cause for the failure of the Federation. This is moreso the case with Lewis who argues that for two years Williams and Manley were embroiled in a battle over the nature of the federal structure. Williams was in favour of a union with a strong centre, while Manley wanted the opposite. Manley was responding to a Jamaican populace which was seemingly apathetic towards a federation. According to Manley, a strong centre would pressure Jamaica into releasing scarce resources, something the country could ill afford in view of the mass poverty which existed. The conflict between Manley and Williams was exploited by Bustamante who, through his election rhetoric, undermined the Federation. Lewis argues that in addition to all of this the Leeward and Windward Islands became dissatisfied with the relations between Trinidad, Jamaica and themselves. This dissatisfaction ultimately led to suspicion when in 1960 the results of a secret meeting (held in Antigua between Trinidad and Jamaica) were withheld from the other countries including the federal prime minister, Grantley Adams. According to Lewis "... the eight now began to assemble under the banner of Sir Grantley Adams who became suspicious of the other two leaders who had nothing to lose by the growing hostilities" (W.A. Lewis 1965: 8).

As a consequence, by 1961, at a conference held in Trinidad no mutual confidence existed among the territories. Jamaica fell out with Trinidad, and Trinidad fell out with the eight (the Leeward and Windward Islands and Barbados). Six of the eight countries were upset with Trinidad for backing down from a previous promise of assisting them economically after independence. Thus, Lewis (1965: 9) contends: "So when in September 1961 Jamaicans voted by a small majority to leave the Federation, relations between the political leaders of Trinidad and those of the eight were at the lowest ebb." Both Mordecai and Lewis conclude that the destruction of the Federation resulted from this perpetual conflict which ultimately reached its zenith with the eruption of tempers. To quote Mordecai (1963: 445), the

"West Indies Federation was finally destroyed by the eruption of anger". As far as Lewis was concerned, "if common sense were to prevail, the departure of Jamaica would have been hailed as a chance to build a strongly centralized federation ... But common sense does not flourish in an atmosphere where everybody is angry with everybody else" (W.A. Lewis 1965:10).

Springer, like Mordecai, while emphasizing differences of personality, also refers to the nationalist conflicts and the parochialism created by colonialism as contributing factors to the demise of the Federation. For Mordecai these factors formed part of the background from whence the personality conflicts arose. However, these factors could have been overcome only if the personalities of the actors had been different. For Springer these factors precipitated the ultimate collapse of the Federation.

He and Mordecai also highlight the prospects of increasing economic prosperity and viability as playing significant roles in determining the lack of commitment by Jamaica to federation. According to Mordecai, following the publication of a pamphlet in 1951 by W.A. Lewis, which argued that the West Indies could develop by inviting foreign investors to set up industries – thus providing the foreign capital, technology and entrepreneurial skills – the Jamaican government embarked on instituting the legal apparatus to encourage such investment. Other positive developments were the expansion of bauxite production and the growth of the tourism industry. As a consequence, whereas Jamaican industrialists had formerly supported the Federation, by 1958 they had changed their position in favour of closer association with the United States as the most viable alternative for the country.

Another factor which underlay the weakness of the Federation, according to Springer, was the fact that the islands were more integrated with Britain than among themselves. Additionally, there was little contact between the Eastern Caribbean and Jamaica until after the advent of air travel.

Etzioni (1965), Bobb (1966) and Lowenthal (1984) are of the view that a critical shortcoming of the Federation was the appalling lack of communication among the countries. Etzioni writes: "the poor communication conditions prevailing among the islands until World War II seemed to have limited interaction among them and contributed to the development of separate identities" (Etzioni 1965:171). He further states that the Federation served the interest of certain ruling groups, had no mass base and depended on a number of charismatic leaders for its survival. Following a similar line of argument, Bobb states that the Federation failed for a number of reasons. First, the conditions for federation never existed. The lack of communication and contact between people allowed for the involvement of only a small section of the people in the process. People, he argues, must want to belong to a nation of multiple states in order for it to succeed. Second, the articulation of the federal idea was 'propagandist' rather than 'agitational'. As a result, the federal idea was preached to people of 'like mind', that is, people who already knew and supported the idea. The idea never really received full discussion among the ordinary working people. Third, the Federation was incapable of uniting the various conflicting classes and social groups which characterized the plural society of the region. There were three main conflicting interests: a white managerial class, a brown bureaucratic class and the black masses. The black masses who saw little economic gain from federation were of the view that the brown bureaucratic elite and the white managerial class were the movement's greatest beneficiaries. Bobb contends:

> ... for insofar as federation becomes a limiting device against disintegrative effects of pluralism for the same reason a federal state would become ineffectual unless it could harmonise and consolidate the society. The contradictory often grotesque social attitudes in the society delayed harmonization and weakened solidarity (Bobb 1966: 257).

For Bobb, therefore, the personality conflicts and poor administration were expressions of these three basic problems. Any attempts at federation would have had to consider the unique geographical and historical nature of the region. These considerations, according to Bobb, were blatantly absent from the conceptual framework of the Federation.

There are a number of other studies on the Federation which use the sociological and personality approaches as outlined in this concise survey. Millette (1969), for example, holds the view that Grantley Adams was the wrong man for the Federation, that only Manley could have made the experiment successful since he was the 'truest' Caribbean man. Additionally, the Federation was dominated by the small islands and administration was far from efficient.

In spite of their contribution to knowledge, these works suffer from a number of shortcomings. Lewis tends to be too descriptive – not getting beyond the surface of the events; that is to say, he sees the manifestations of the problems as the cause of the problems. His analysis is divorced from the historical, social, political and economic reality of the region at the time. As a consequence, he arrives at the rather questionable conclusion that exploding tempers and a lack of commonsense prevented the formation of a stronger federation of the Eastern Caribbean after the seccession of Jamaica.

Although Springer and Mordecai represent obvious improvements over Lewis in terms of analysis, they too occasionally fall prey to detail and description of personalities which ultimately reflect the social environment. Etzioni and Bobb, while trying to transcend the limitations of the personality approach, sometimes tend to be too general. The shortcomings of the writers are reflective of approaches which could have benefited from cross-fertilization. Perhaps the greatest failing of the writers is their lack of a clear theoretical framework, which could have generated general propositions explaining the failure of the Federation, rather than having a multiplicity of apparently separate and oftentimes disconnected points.

Overall, there are two major issues which could account for the failure of the Federation. First, there is the historically insular development of the territories which militated against the creation of a common identity and, by implication, an ideology of regionalism; secondly, there is the conceptual framework of federation – the idea of federation being used as a means of attaining constitutional self-government – which was not concerned with the reproduction of federation as an end in itself.

In relation to the first issue, it is important to note that all of the writers conceded the insular nature of the region before and after the federal experiment. This was due to the nature of the administration of the colonies of the region under British colonialism. As Gordon Lewis explains, "colonial rule in the West Indies has always been decentralized, separating island from island by means of separate administration" (G. Lewis 1968: 89). Although the colonial era was characterized by the rise of West Indian nationalism, this was never strong enough to overcome the weaknesses of fragmentation. When conflicts emerged they always seemed to manifest parochial interests of the parties involved and were therefore incapable of being resolved in a collective spirit. Etzioni is correct when he states that the Federation did not develop "the ideological, economic or military power necessary to counter secessionist attempts" (Etzioni 1965:138).

The implications of this situation dictated that for any strong form of regional integration to succeed it would have to be conceived in such a way as to allow for institutional development aimed at overcoming these divisions. There would be need to develop a strong commitment to federation, which in turn would require that federation be seen both as a means to an end and also as an end in itself. This leads to the second point which is that the idea of federation arose, principally, as a means of achieving self-government and not as an end in itself. As Payne cogently puts it, federation had "always been seen in the West Indies as a means to an end, literally as a gateway to independence, and never, therefore, as an end and an ideal in its own right" (Payne 1980:19).

Manley made this point absolutely clear at the Montego Bay Conference. According to him:

> I say here we are all in a sea of world conditions, stormy and hazardous in the extreme, each huddled in some little craft of our own. Some hardly have oars and only a few have accomplished a rudimentary

sail to take them along ... If we won't leave our little boats and get into a larger vessel which is able to carry us to the goal of our ambition then I say without hesitation we are doomed ... and history will condemn us (Manley 1948: 57-62).

In 1956 Williams stated:

Whether federation is more costly or less costly, wether federation is more efficient or less efficient, federation is inescapable if the British Caribbean are to cease to parade themselves to the twentieth century as eighteenth century anachronisms. It is this point of view that I have frequently stated, that any federation is better than no federation (Williams 1956:11-12).

Federation got full British support as expressed in a British Colonial Office report of 1947 which expressed the view that it was impossible for the small and isolated territories to achieve full self-government on their own (Springer 1962). But this was also a way for Britain to be rid of the now burdensome administration of the colonies. Thus, Thomas (1979: 284) notes that federation was "... simply a way of getting around the so-called difficulties of dealing administratively with a large number of small communities" (Thomas 1979: 284).

Conflict, however, existed over the nature of the federal structure. This lack of consensus reflected differences in both the perception of the region and commitment to federation. There were basically two opposing views of federation: one championed the need for a weak centre while the other favoured the opposite. These positions were most clearly articulated by Manley and Williams, respectively.

Williams held the view that the Federation should assume full dominion status which he suggested for 22 April 1960. In a publication entitled *Economics of Nationhood*, Williams set out the structure of the Federation. He argued that it should be based on a clear-cut comprehensive conception aimed at:

1. national independence and security
2. basic human freedoms including freedom of religious worship
3. the development of a national spirit
4. the economic development and integration of the area.

Williams further suggested increasing the powers of the federal government to intervene in the financial and policy areas of each country. In addition, the federal government would have the last say in the formulation of legislation and matters affecting planning and development of all kinds.

Manley adopted the opposite position, preferring to restrict federal powers. He suggested that issues of industrial development, power to levy income tax, excise duties and consumption be removed from the control of the federal government. He also argued that if the territories of the Eastern Caribbean so desired, a constitutional formula should be adopted to allow the federal government to have a greater say in the running of their affairs. Jamaica, he argued, was unequivocally opposed to such interventions.

These two conflicting approaches resulted in a split within the federal movement. Trinidad's proposals were in keeping with the original ones as advocated by the early nationalists such as Marryshow and Cipriani. They were supported by federalist stalwarts such as Grantley Adams who became the first federal prime minister. However, many thought that the Williams proposals were nothing more than naive idealism. Above all, the smaller territories saw the proposals outlined in the *Economics of Nationhood* as reducing them to nothing more than county councils (Williams 1959). The result of this was that leaders failed to agree on a formula for a federal structure.

The conflicting positions of Manley and Williams were the result of different perceptions of the region. Historically, Trinidad had been closely linked to the Eastern Caribbean and was involved in the federal debates from the outset. Jamaica on the other hand, being geographically and politically isolated from the rest of the region, only became involved in the federation debates during the 1940s. While it is true that ultimately the Federation represented a means to an end, for Trinidad, as perhaps for most of the other countries of the Eastern Caribbean, it had a deeper emotional significance. Hence, Williams comments that: "only a powerful and centrally directed economic coordination and interdependence can create the true foundation of a *nation* (writer's emphasis)" (Williams 1959:11). The variations in support for these two positions indicated that the notion of a regional identity was not well developed during the federal era. Neither did the Federation follow any clear ideology of regionalism which would have acted as a base and guide to action.

Notwithstanding the support for federation, Lowenthal notes that by 1960, when Prime Minister Norman Manley became convinced that Jamaica could go it alone, the federalist idea became less of an attraction. Manley's change of heart had been, to a large degree, the result of Jamaica's increased economic prosperity and the prospects of independent economic viability (Lowenthal 1984). But to be fair, Manley's decision to 'go it alone' was also conditioned by the views of a section of the PNP leadership who had been less than enthusiastic about the Federation. Therefore, Manley's lack of zeal for the Federation was not for want of commitment to regionalism, but the result of internal political factors and new ideas about the viability of small states at the time. The idea of separate statehood, argues Lowenthal, was further to influence Trinidad's decision to follow the Jamaican withdrawal.

Trinidad, like Jamaica, had also been experiencing an economic boom as a result of increased earnings from oil. By the mid-1950s Trinidad had become one of the fastest growing economies in the world (Mordecai 1963). The notion of economic viability based on the concept of a particular size had been shattered. Hence, Trinidad's movement towards independence was followed by Guyana and Barbados. As Lowenthal notes, given this revolutionary departure from the past, "no theoretical justification remained to deny self-government to any Caribbean territory" (Lowenthal 1984:113-14).

Evidence of Manley's change of mood occurred in the inter-governmental conference of 1960 at which he made a speech which placed Jamaica's support for the Federation in doubt. Manley's views were also conditioned by the strong anti-federation campaigns of Bustamante who appealed to the nationalist sentiments of Jamaicans and suggested that a federation could not improve the living conditions of the people. The referendum of 1961 revealed the lack of zeal with which Manley approached federation. A considerably smaller number of supporters of Manley's People's National Party (PNP) than of Bustamante's Jamaica Labour Party (JLP) turned out to vote (Millette 1969). This was especially striking in the PNP's strongest constituencies. Therefore in the end, a strong anti-Federation climate both within some sections of the PNP and within the JLP, along with a new perspective on small states and economic and development, contributed to Manley's reluctant decision that Jamaica should leave the Federation.

Although Trinidad had proposed a unitary state with the other eight countries after the Jamaican withdrawal, internal party sentiment of Williams' People's National Movement was against the idea because of the economic cost to be borne by Trinidad. Internal party conflicts and continuous controversy between Trinidad and the eight made further thoughts of federation less acceptable to Williams (Millette 1969). The prospects of independent economic development ultimately encouraged Trinidad to go to independence alone. As Coard puts it (1978: 69), Trinidad had come to realize that "the world's concept of the size required of an independent nation ... [had been] altered".

After the withdrawal of Trinidad from the ill-fated federation with the eight, a federation of the eight themselves was proposed. Initially, Barbados was reluctant to conclude constitutional arrangements for independence because: (i) it was not willing to make the establishment of federation a more difficult task; (ii) there was concern over the inability of the country to provide its own security; (iii) there was still the underlying view that a country so small could not be viable on its own. However, conflicts between Barbados and the other islands along with the perception that Barbados would have to bear the bulk of the economic cost of federation created some doubts in the mind of Errol Barrow, the then premier, about the idea. Given these tensions along with the possibility of independent viability, Barbados concluded constitutional arrangements to receive its independence on 30 November 1966. This action brought the curtain down on any further attempts at forming a regional federation.

From Federation to CARIFTA to CARICOM

Even though the Federation failed, efforts at bringing about integration within the region still continued. Such efforts were initially led by Williams who continuously championed the idea of an economic community. But it was only during the second half of the 1960s that actual steps were taken to realize such a goal. This was partly in response to a publication by William Demas entitled *The Economics of Development in Small Countries with Special Reference to the Caribbean* in which the argument was made that the countries of the region should pursue economic integration in order to overcome the development limitations imposed by their small size. In this publication, Demas recognized the existence of structural deficiencies in the countries as being the main cause of high unemployment; a dual economy with a high-wage sector in the mineral and manufacturing economy, resulting in the flow of labour from agriculture to these areas; the poor use of local resources; an underdeveloped tourist industry because of lack of linkages within the economies; and a situation where foreign investors were responding to investment incentives, created by the regional governments, by the setting up of screwdriver type industries. He concluded that failure to transform the economies of the region to make them become more viable entities was a direct result of their small size. As Payne puts it, the thrust of Demas' argument was:

> the smallness of the domestic market imposed sharp limits on the process of import substitution industrialization and thus removed the option of balanced growth, incorporating a roughly equal mixture of export stimulation and import substitution, a goal which could only be achieved by large continental countries (Payne 1980: 58).

As a result of this situation, small countries were forced to produce a small number of manufactures for export to world markets, but this in itself was beset by a number of obstacles which lowered the competitiveness of the products. Demas therefore identified two options for the small countries to choose from if they were to achieve industrial development: (i) full economic integration with large countries, similar to Puerto Rico's relationship with the United States; (ii) integration with similar countries within the same geographical area. Demas chose the latter, arguing that by integrating the

43

economies of the region there would be the elimination of excess capacity in the existing manufacturing industry and the stimulation of new industries which could become more viable given the expanded market (Payne 1980). In reality, Demas was calling for a collective approach to import substitution.

A point which is worth noting at this stage is that Demas' approach was vastly different from that advocated by the University of the West Indies economists who, in 1964, under the aegis of the Trinidadian and Jamaican governments, were commissioned to conduct studies on regional economic integration. The University team published a number of papers and books – the most celebrated being *The Dynamics of West Indian Integration* by C.Y. Thomas and Havelock Brewster, produced in 1967. The University team's proposals were rejected on the grounds that they were too naive and radical, although some effort was made to salvage some of the ideas by incorporating aspects of production integration into the Caribbean Free Trade Association Agreement (CARIFTA) (Payne 1980). Thus, the signatories to CARIFTA chose to pursue Demas' approach which followed the neoclassical economic perspective, not seeking to question or change the structure of the regional economies.

Although this Agreement came into effect in August 1968, events dating from 1965 led to its development. In 1965 the governments of Antigua, Barbados and Guyana responded to the idea of an economic community by agreeing to the creation of a Free Trade Association by 1966. In 1966, the Hunte Committee, named after a prominent Barbadian businessman, Kenneth Hunte, was appointed to tour the region to convince regional leaders to take action in order to start a free trade association (Payne 1980). In 1967, Forbes Burnham, prime minister of Guyana, met with Eric Williams to convince Trinidad to join the Free Trade Association. The announcement of a free trade association had caught the region by surprise – in particular Trinidad's Eric Williams, who had been one of the earliest and strongest advocates of post-federation economic integration. Williams must have been displeased by such reticence on the part of the three countries. In stressing the necessity for Trinidad to join the association, Burnham stated:

> Either we weld ourselves into a regional grouping serving primarily Caribbean needs, or lacking a common positive policy, have our various territories and nations drawn hither and thither into, and by, other large territories where the peculiar problems of the Caribbean are lost and where we become the objects of neocolonialist exploitation, and achieve the pitiable status of international mendicants ... Either we integrate or we perish, unwept, unhonoured (Burnham 1970: 246-47).

Here again history repeats itself, as these views are reminiscent of those articulated by Norman Manley during the Montego Bay Conference of 1947. In this quotation and in the works of Demas there exists a congruency in rationale for both the Federation and economic integration to overcome the limitations imposed by small size. Economic integration, like federation, had been advocated as a means to an end and not as an end in itself. This point is even more vividly exemplified in the efforts to get the LDCs to join CARIFTA.

One of the central concerns of the LDCs has always been that of securing short and long term financing for development. Prospects for such financing would be used to convince the LDCs to join CARIFTA. According to Payne "a Caribbean Development Bank financed chiefly by contributions from metropolitan countries and the larger Caribbean states but geared specifically to their needs was manifestly attractive bait to hold before the LDCs" (Payne 1980: 95).

Thus in 1968 CARIFTA, comprising a group of countries pursuing pragmatic interests but holding the view that being in such an association made them more viable, was born. It was however for such reasons, economic pragmatism and continued individual interests, that for the four years of its existence CARIFTA became afflicted by perpetual conflict and intense rivalry. For instance, in 1968 both Barbados and Jamaica rejected a proposal by Trinidad to make British West Indian Airways (BWIA) the regional air carrier. BWIA had been purchased by the government of Trinidad from British Overseas Air Corporation (BOAC) when it ended operations in the Caribbean. Trinidad, which purchased the airline without consultation with other Caribbean counterparts, had started to incur extremely heavy losses from its operations. The formation of CARIFTA was therefore an opportunity for the Trinidad government to make the airline a regional one thereby reducing the costs of operation (Payne 1980). Although a working party set up at the Fourth Heads of Government Conference to examine the matter was unanimously in favour of making the airline regional, since above all it made economic sense, at the Ministerial Conference the idea was rejected. The main reason for the rejection was that Jamaica had already embarked on setting up its own airline, while Barbados was in the process of doing the same. In both cases the two countries were using national airlines to help in the development of their individual tourist industries (Payne 1980). Trinidad was displeased with the decision and even threatened to secede from the movement.

Another issue which caused much dissatisfaction within the movement was the growing trade polarization in favour of the MDCs. Between 1968 and 1970 the MDCs witnessed increases in exports from EC$96 million to

EC$158 million, an increase of 65 per cent. Jamaica benefited most from such increases. In response to complaints by the LDCs about the need to address the imbalance, the MDCs blamed the LDC for a lack of entrepreneurial drive. As a result of a perceived intransigence by the MDCs, the LDCs opposed suggestions by the MDCs for deepening the movement. As far as they were concerned, deepening the integration process would only worsen the already polarized situation and work to the benefit of the MDCs. For example, deepening which meant the harmonization of fiscal incentives and the implementation of a common external tariff could cause the LDC markets to be more open to the exports of the MDCs and also place them at a disadvantage in attracting foreign investment (Payne 1980). But neither was Jamaica interested in deepening the integration process. Prime Minister Shearer, who succeeded Bustamante, made this point very clear on numerous occasions and insisted that Jamaica was simply interested in economic co-operation. He proposed instead the widening of the movement to include non-English speaking territories, as this would widen the tariff free market size. Guyana, Trinidad and Barbados were, however, firmly in favour of the deepening process. As a result, CARIFTA became split along two conflicting viewpoints regarding its development.

Another issue which aggravated the existing tensions within the movement and served to reinforce the observation that the movement suffered from parochialism and lacked ideological cohesion was its failure to reach consensus on a common policy towards the European Economic Community (EEC). In 1969, regional governments realizing the imminence of Britain's entry into the European Economic Community, sent a delegation to Britain to lobby the case of the region for special consideration (Payne 1980). Although the Seventh Heads of Government Conference later agreed on the need for a collective approach to the matter, where a single form of relationship was to be negotiated, there was still dispute over which option would be most suitable. There were basically three options of association, Guyana and Trinidad preferring one type while Jamaica preferred another. In each case the choice of option was based on the perceived benefits that could be derived individually. In addition, there was also the case of the LDCs which, because of their associated status with Britain, were eligible for the most advantageous form of association within the group. They were subsequently persuaded to forego such an option in favour of the collective one. In the final analysis it was Britain which made the decision on the type of option for association. What was perhaps most startling about these series of events was the fact that Jamaica had been secretly negotiating with the European Economic Community for a new type of arrangement which suited their immediate economic needs (Payne 1980).

As a result of this perpetual conflict, by the 1970s, in spite of the progress made in the expansion of trade, the continued viability of CARIFTA had been threatened. Unlike the Federation though, this movement was not to fall into a state of disrepair. ~~*saved somewhat*~~

In 1972 the integration movement got a fillip from the accession to power of the People's National Party (PNP) in Jamaica, under the leadership of Michael Manley. Michael, like his father Norman, made no secret of the fact that he was an unrepentant integrationist (Payne 1980). In 1970 Manley had published an article in *Foreign Affairs* which echoed strong sentiments in favour of regional economic integration. In this paper Manley emphasized the economic benefits that Jamaica and the region could achieve from closer regional integration. Manley's well articulated position and rhetoric became a morale booster for the integration movement. In 1972 Demas, who was then Secretary General of CARIFTA, published a booklet entitled "From CARIFTA to the Caribbean Community" in which he outlined a policy for the deepening of the integration process. These ideas would to a large degree influence the formation and structure of the new integration movement. He suggested increased economic cooperation through a common market and an extension to the areas of functional cooperation. The deepening of regional integration therefore rested on the same basic premise as CARIFTA: "CARIFTA and CARICOM have been designed in the first instance to overcome the constraints upon the economies of the region imposed by the small size" (Payne 1980: 187).

CARICOM has three basic objectives: (i) economic cooperation through the Caribbean Common Market; (ii) coordination of foreign policy among independent member states; (iii) functional or non-functional cooperation in areas such as health, education, sea and air transport, culture, etc. The supreme organ of the Community is the Conference of Heads of Government. It is made up of prime ministers, and in the case of Guyana and Montserrat, executive president and chief minister, respectively. The final authority on policy matters of the community rests with this Conference.

The principal organ of the Common Market is called the Common Market Council. It is responsible for the smooth running and development of the Common Market. There are several institutions of CARICOM responsible for formulating policies in relation to functional cooperation. Each member state is represented on each institution by a minister of government. The institutions are in the form of standing committees on health, education, science, technology, foreign affairs, agriculture, mines, energy and natural resources, transport, finance and labour. There are also associate institutions of the Community which form the main planks of functional cooperation. They include the Caribbean Examinations Council

(CXC), the Caribbean Meteorological Association (CMO), the Council of Legal Education (CLE), the University of the West Indies (UWI), the University of Guyana (UG) and the West Indies Shipping Corporation (WISCO). The Community Secretariat is organized into five divisions, namely trade and agriculture, economics and industry, functional cooperation, legal, and general services and administration.

There are foruteen countries in CARICOM. These are St. Lucia, St. Vincent, Grenada, Antigua and Barbuda, St. Christopher and Nevis, Montserrat, Belize and Dominica – classified as LDCs; Barbados, Trinidad and Tobago, Guyana, Jamaica and Suriname, the most recent member – classified as MDCs. The Bahamas, which makes up the fourteenth member, has not been slotted into either of these categories.

In 1981 a subgroup comprising the LDCs from the Eastern Caribbean formed themselves into an association called the Organization of Eastern Caribbean States (OECS). The formation of this group was a response to the skewed level of economic development which had come to characterize the movement.

Unlike the Federation, CARICOM has managed to survive. However, like the Federation and CARIFTA, the movement has been characterized by tremendous conflict and instability. The following chapter attempts to examine some of the experiences of CARICOM with a view to offering an explanation as to why this conflict and instability persist.

CHAPTER 4

CARICOM: Its Shortcomings and the Case for an Ideology of Regionalism

The spectre of instability and conflict has over the years threatened the viability of the regional integration movement. So persistent has this situation been that commentators and actors of the process all seem to share the view that the regional movement is in a state of crisis.

According to Hippolyte-Manigat (1979), regional newspapers have reached a consensus on the crisis in CARICOM. The *Barbados Advocate News* of 26 February 1977 castigated the member countries of the Community because the Treaty of Chaguaramas was "honoured more in breach than observance". The Jamaican *Gleaner* in its editorial of 10 May 1977 lamented that "the future of CARICOM looks bleak to say the least", while, in a similar negative but even more dramatic vein, the *Trinidad Express* in an article published on 9 December 1977 stated that "CARICOM was no longer vibrant but gasping for its survival". The same paper, on 12 February 1978, expressed the despondent opinion that "CARICOM deserved a decent burial".

Politicians, too, have been just as pessimistic in their prognosis for the movement. In 1976, Guyana's Desmond Hoyte declared that "a pall of gloom is now hanging over the Caribbean Unity, and the objectives of CARICOM and its people are in danger" (Hippolyte-Manigat 1977). Similar comments have come from Austin Bramble, former chief minister of Montserrat, as well as the late Dr. Eric Williams, former prime minister of Trinidad, to name but a few (Eckstein 1978).

Leading regional interest groups have also expressed their doubts about the viability of CARICOM. Lennie Saint Hill, former president of the Barbados Chamber of Commerce, stated quite categorically on 26 May 1977 that CARICOM was a "palpable failure" and that it "is dead and only an incalculable indecency of opportunism denies its burial" (Hippolyte-Manigat 1977). Indeed, similar comments were shared in 1978 by Avis Henriques, former president of the Jamaica Manufacturers' Association (JMA) who admitted that "the bond of brotherhood" in CARICOM has proven to be fragile and CARICOM itself is floundering" (Hippolyte-Manigat 1977). These views although expressed during the latter half of the 1970s, a period of both regional and international economic and political turbulence, persisted, albeit in a moderate form, throughout the 1980s. In 1983, Alister McIntyre, former secretary general of CARICOM painted a gloomy picture of the regional integration movement, when he stated that "the regional integration movement is in deep trouble" (McIntyre 1984). He further suggested that there was need for urgent action as the process of decision making, in addition to the lack of commitment to the process, was plunging the movement into disarray.

In 1984, three researchers from the Mona campus of the University of the West Indies, in an article entitled "Jamaica and the Economic Crisis in CARICOM", presented an analysis of the experience of CARICOM since its inception, and concluded that CARICOM was in a state of crisis, and that "while a deepening of integration is desirable, a lack of consensus and political unity makes this extremely unlikely" (Bernal et al. 1984).

As if to suggest that the time had come for regional leaders to mend their ways and employ a new strategy to tackle the crisis faced by the regional movement, an article in the *Caribbean Contact* (July 1987) advised that the CARICOM Heads of Government meeting "will be in grave danger of flogging the poor trade horse to death if they meet again in July 1987, to quarrel over the failure of some to abide by the Nassau Agreement".

The foregoing testimonies, while being a sad commentary on the persistent problems faced by CARICOM are, more importantly, a reflection of the inadequacy of the integration movement. CARICOM is really the epitome of this integration movement in its formal sense, as it is the practical manifestation of the integration idea. Thus, Hippolyte-Manigat (1979:4) is correct when she argues that the crisis is one which "puts in evidence the structural inefficiency of a specific framework for welcoming, beyond functional achievements, a quality of collective life, an ideal of unity for the peoples of the region". It is for such a reason that there is need for a "reassessment of the very *raison d'être* of CARICOM as a model for building Caribbean unity through integration" (Demas 1974:5). The problem is therefore not simply structural but also conceptual.

Following such a line of thinking, the ensuing discussion shall attempt to show that the regional integration movement is weak and unstable. This is mainly because it is guided by a philosophy of economic pragmatism which sees a plurality of interests converging in the hope of achieving unity. As a consequence of this philosophy, regional integration is undermined as national and sectional interests are advanced over regional ones. Additionally, conflict arises over priorities and objectives because of differing approaches to the notion of regionalism. The formulation as well as the implementation of policies by member countries at both the national and regional level are, hence, not based on a system of ideas or ideology which recognizes the deepening and consolidating of the integration process itself as an inextricable part of the development of each individual territory. In a region made up of competing underdeveloped capitalist countries with a legacy of insularity and the hegemony of two superpowers, the United Kingdom and the United States of America, such an arrangement is bound to have more than its fair share of conflicts.

In order to demonstrate the claim made here, the remainder of this discourse shall focus on some of the experiences of CARICOM during the latter part of the 1970s through the 1980s, with greater emphasis on the former period. The discussion shall be confined to an examination of:

1. the conceptual framework of CARICOM, the Treaty of Chaguaramas

2. experiences within the common market

3. the co-ordination of foreign policy

4. sectoral interests within the movement.

The CARICOM Treaty — Ramifications for Integration

The Treaty of Chaguaramas embodies the basic philosophy which underlies the regional integration movement. The Treaty falls into two sections, the main Treaty containing provisions relating to foreign policy co-ordination and areas of functional co-operation; and the Common Market Annex containing provisions relating to the economic integration aspect of the Community (Geiser 1977).

What this means in reality, according to Geiser, is that there are two separate treaties, bringing together two separate organizations — the Community *stricto sensu* and the Common Market. The question which ultimately arises relates to why was the Treaty not made into a single basic one since "the Community's objectives of economic integration, foreign policy co-ordination and functional co-operation are so closely united with one another" (Geiser 1977:33).

The answer simply underscores the thinking behind the movement, namely, that it sought to incorporate in some unit the different interests which individual member countries had in the movement. The three major objectives were not of equal importance to each territory (Geiser 1977). Some were primarily concerned with economic integration while others were attracted by the benefits to be derived from functional co-operation. Hence, from the outset, the agreement was not exactly one of collective interest, rather it represented an attempt to converge the competing individual interests into a collective. The former presupposes the existence of an ideology shared by the collective, the whole possessing more importance than the parts. The latter is characterized by competing individual ideologies with similar interests, the whole taking precedence only insofar as it fulfils the interests of the individual parts. In this case, a member country is likely to breach the agreement, even at the expense of the collective, because an individual need is not being fulfilled.

Another ramification of the Treaty relates to the fact that it makes the question of priorities within the movement a difficult one to agree on. Indeed, this has negative implications for the formulation of policy since to be successful it requires the consensus of member countries.

Perhaps of even greater concern is the fact that the Treaty is couched in such general terms that it encourages delinquency. One case in point relates to the issue of production integration. This is dealt with under Articles 45, 46 and 47. Article 45 provides for a long term perspective plan to promote maximum complementarity between industries and the economic sector of member states (Geiser 1977). Article 46 aims to promote regional industrial programming with the following objectives in mind:

(a) the greater utilization of the raw materials of the Common Market;

(b) the creation of production linkages both within and between the national economies of the Common Market;

(c) to minimize product differentiation and achieve economies of large scale production, consistent with the limitations of market size;

(d)   the encouragement of greater efficiency in industrial production;

(e)   the promotion of exports to markets both within and outside the Common Market;

(f)   an equitable distribution of benefits of industrialization, paying particular attention to the need to locate more industries in "Less Developed States" (Geiser 1977).

Finally, Article 47 talks about a policy which seeks to promote joint development of resources for increased utilization of these resources within the Common Market and collaboration in the promotion of research. In no way does the Treaty speak directly to the issue of production integration, thereby committing members to the fulfilment of such an objective. However, the articles are enough to satisfy Demas that the Treaty encompasses the realization of the University of the West Indies concept of "production integration". According to Demas, the critics fail to understand "that the provisions of a treaty must be couched in somewhat general and 'permissive' terms" (Demas quoted in Payne 1980:184). But some critics have sought to show that there are two sides to the issue, for as Payne argues (1980:72) "flexibility is one side of the coin that has wooliness on the other". In fact, he is adamant that:

> the harsh political truth is that the CARICOM Treaty was couched in general terms, precisely because this was the only level at which agreement could be reached between Governments on the range of issues which Demas and the Secretariat wanted the Treaty to embrace. The aim, bluntly stated, [was] to postpone the struggle and go for a superficial unanimity over a wider number of subjects (Payne 1980:185).

This point brings the discussion full circle to the original contention that the philosophy behind CARICOM heralded economic pragmatism and a convergence of a plurality of interests. However, such a philosophy of integration for the region lies at the heart of the difficulties experienced within CARICOM.

Integration within the Common Market

One of the most conflict-ridden areas within CARICOM is that of economic integration. Economic integration is the principal objective of the Community and it is provided for by a Common Market regime outlined in the Annex of the Treaty (Treaty establishing the Caribbean Community 1973). There are five spheres of activity which constitute the Common Market arrangements. These are trade liberalization, the Common External Tariff (CET) and the Common Protective Policy (CPP), factor mobility, co-ordination of economic policies and production integration. The success of economic integration is therefore based on achievements in these spheres of activity. However, progress in these areas has been slow and in many cases absent. Disagreements, broken promises and self-interest compounded by the negative effects brought on by changes in the world economy have resulted in extreme strains and tensions within the movement.

The free trade regime, which outlines the rules of fair competition and specifies the products which are subject to quantitative restrictions or import duties, was re-established in chapter 3 of the Common Market Annex much the same as it was under the CARIFTA Agreement (Payne 1980). The only changes of noticeable significance relate to extra concessions made to the LDCs. These include the extension of the period afforded them for removing duties on the items on the reserve list; the right to use government aids to subsidize their exports to MDCs with the exception of Barbados, and to purchase supplies from their own producers on other than strictly commercial grounds; and the reduction of the percentage of local "value added" required to qualify a product for free trade. Although the region has experienced a large degree of liberalized trade, it does not follow that such was the outcome of CARICOM, since this was the case even before the signing of the CARIFTA Treaty. Admittedly, intra-regional trade did improve since the implementation of a free trade area and although this cannot with certainty be attributed to trade liberalization, the fact is that from the very beginning 90 per cent of the intra-regional trade was free of import duties and quantitative restrictions (Hippolyte-Manigat 1979). Hence, the value of intra-regional trade skyrocketed from US $35.5 million in 1968 to US $247.7 million in 1974, an increase of 700 per cent.

Nevertheless, such increases are not spectacular since the ratio of intra-regional trade to gross domestic product is still very small (Appendix I). Indeed, this point becomes clearer when one examines the structure of global importations of which intra-regional trade stood at only 4 per cent in 1968, 7.19 per cent in 1974 and 8.19 per cent in 1975 (Appendixes II, III).

Even after achieving some success in the area of intra-regional trade no attempt was made to change the structure of these economies and the way they were incorporated into the world economy. According to Hippolyte-Manigat (1979), the movement was not trade creation oriented, but continued to be engaged in trade diversion. The region continued to be a depository for branch plants of multi-national corporations (MNCs). It meant, therefore, that in attempting to attract "screwdriver" industries, regionally produced goods, except for some agricultural and petroleum products, were destined to have only small amounts of regional value added (Thomas 1979). In an effort to sustain their individual national economies and in order to maintain investment competitiveness, member countries exploited the weakness of the Basic Materials List.

The Basic Materials List was drawn up with the intention of developing regional industry by extending preferential treatment to goods which contained materials originating from the region (Thomas 1979). According to Payne, the "rules of origin" is a serious weakness of the CARICOM Treaty since the Basic Materials List is too long and includes products which could either be produced within the region, and/or for which regional substitutes are or can become available (Payne 1980). It means therefore that countries could import, under the free trade regime, goods with minimal "value added", thus defeating the whole objective of the regime.

Although this problem was mitigated by the implementation of the New Origin System in 1981, which measures eligibility by the degree of processing which occurs in their production, countries of the OECS are still free to apply value added criteria to a number of commodities (Payne 1980). In addition, there is also the fact that the Basic Materials List allows certain imported materials used in the manufacture of commodities to be treated as local materials for the calculation of value added, a situation which discourages the utilization of local inputs thus inhibiting the growth of backward linkages in production (Payne 1980).

In spite of the fact that intra-regional trade has increased and there has been the adoption of the free trade regime, the region has experienced a significant degree of trade polarization favourable to the MDCs (Appendixes IV, V). The process of liberalization of exchanges was supposed to distribute the trade benefits facilitated by the provisions of the regime. However, as C.Y. Thomas notes, capitalist development is always uneven, hence polarization of trade within CARICOM is inevitable (Thomas 1979). The problem also stems from the fact that the Common Market, because of its pragmatic nature, is too loose and unchecked. In other words, for a free trade area to be of success, there must be "the implementation of a dirigiste policy and intervention of a supranational authority capable of dividing trade production and trade distribution among the participants" (Hippolyte-Manigat 1979:10).

In addition, a closer integration of the region into a single unit would have resulted in less inequality and a greater distribution of national revenues between peoples by virtue of a distributive policy. But the ramifications of this factor might also result in the strict acceptance by the MDCs of the "special disposition of the Treaty favourable to the LDCs, even at the risk of a voluntary lessening of their own revenues" (Hippolyte-Manigat 1979:10).

In other words, concerns with individual interest would have to be subsumed to the larger regional interest. Since the Treaty eschews this type of regionalism there are no mechanisms in place, of an ethical nor technical nature, to ensure strict observance of its dispositions. Therefore, according to Hippolyte-Manigat (1980:13), this situation has become one in which every country is "interpreting and fulfilling its commitments according to its own interests, introducing deleterious practices aimed at getting more from the system than it is putting into it".

A case in point was during 1975 when the Jamaica Manufacturers' Association (JMA) denounced its CARICOM partners for not abiding by the rules of the Treaty (Hippolyte-Manigat 1979). They highlighted the fact that Trinidad and Barbados were not purchasing potatoes from Jamaica but they were importing them from extra-regional countries. Subsequently, however, Jamaica was found guilty of breaching the Treaty when the Government on 12 October placed all CARICOM imports under a licensing system. In seeking to rationalize such a move, P.J. Patterson, Minister of Industry, Foreign Affairs and Trade declared before the House of Representatives in Jamaica that the measure was a mere monitoring mechanism and not any form of quantitative restriction. It was "a means of forcing Jamaican importers to make rational decisions concerning their imports placed in the limits of their foreign exchange allocations" (Hippolyte-Manigat 1979:39). Given the foregoing, one should therefore not be surprised to find that member countries have sought as far as possible to manipulate the "rules of origin" to their own individual benefit.

Incidentally, C.Y. Thomas's point that the "rules of origin" was deliberately formulated in the way it was to allow countries to "secure the position of the simple fabrication, screw-driver, branch plant firms" cannot be ignored (Thomas 1979). The fact of the matter is that the structure of the regional economies remains predisposed to this type of industrial development (Girvan and Jefferson 1976). This type of development not only creates more divisions due to the competition involved in attracting foreign investments, but also as Best, Bernal and so many others have argued, it increases the vulnerability of these countries to the ups and downs of the world economy (see Bernal et al. 1984).

Ironically, although the CARICOM agreement was conceived to cushion CARICOM countries from the shocks brought on by changes in the world economy, these changes have only showed up the weakness of the movement. For instance, in 1975, due to adverse economic difficulties resulting mainly from a down-turn in the world economy, the Jamaican government placed all CARICOM imports under a licensing system, thereby ending the previously privileged treatment of CARICOM goods. Guyana, also affected by such a crisis, reacted by placing all goods under a special licence, requiring sanction from the Ministry of Trade and Consumer Protection before importation could be allowed. From 1976, all of the imports were monitored by a block currency quota system which enabled importers to obtain licences for only 70 per cent of the value of what they brought in 1976. Jamaica followed such a system, fixed at Jamaican J$850 million and J$600 million in 1976 and 1977, respectively (Hippolyte-Manigat 1979). This had a dramatic effect on intra-regional trade, which fell in absolute terms. For example, in 1976 Trinidadian exports to Jamaica fell by 34 per cent compared to 1975. Jamaican imports from CARICOM in 1977 decreased by 40.7 per cent compared to 1976, that is, from J$34.5 million in 1976 to J$20.5 million in 1977. Barbados, Trinidad and Guyana were the hardest hit by this situation. In Barbados 25 per cent (or over 800) of the garment workers, who constitute one of the largest sectors of the economy, were laid off. In Trinidad massive industrial conflict erupted when between 3,500 and 7,000 garment workers were axed. In 1977, Trinidad experienced a 90 per cent decline in exports to Jamaica and an 85 per cent decline in exports to Guyana. According to Hippolyte-Manigat, the garment industry in Trinidad was developed partly on the firm assurance that Jamaica would be a major accessible market. However, with the continued decline in sales to Jamaica, the Trinidad Manufacturers' Association (TMA) sought extra-regional markets.

Trinidad's response to this crisis was to further plunge regional economic integration into even greater doubts. In 1977, Dr. Eric Williams announced that Trinidad would no longer pursue a policy of "unreciprocal generosity" and "unilateral understanding" but one which was to be later dubbed "tit-for-tat" (Hippolyte-Manigat 1979). In that year he set up a committee which also acquired the title of "Tit-for-Tat Committee", aimed at combating the trade restrictions imposed by member countries. What resulted was a recommendation that 48 categories of CARICOM products be placed under restriction and an import control policy developed which would echo the sentiments that Trinidad would take remedial action to ensure the viability of its local industries. This policy of "tit-for-tat" represented a deviation from Trinidad's earlier professed policy which saw itself as the big brother and protector of the integration movement.

The foregoing scenario paints a clear picture. The fact of the matter is that crises in the world economy, instead of sparking off a sense of solidarity in CARICOM, weaken it. Because the integration movement does not give ultimate priority to collective interests over individual ones, member countries, when faced with a crisis, adopt measures which are designed to protect their own individual national interests, even at the expense of other countries.

The pre-eminence accorded national concerns over regional ones accounts in great part for the lack of agreement by CARICOM member countries on the question of foreign investment. Article 44 of the Annex states that:

> member states shall keep under review the question of ownership and control of resources with a view to increasing the extent of national participation in their economies and working towards the adoption as far as possible of a common policy on foreign investment (Treaty 1973:11).

According to Payne (1980), the clause represents a real contradiction, since it reflects a situation in which there is an attempt to continue to attract foreign investment, while simultaneously there is a growing awareness of the need to "contain its adverse effects". The movement has therefore found it difficult to reach a consensus on foreign investment, since some member countries feel that they would be disadvantaged by such a policy. This is the feeling shared by the LDCs in particular, which rejected the Draft Agreement on Foreign Investment and the Development of Technology submitted at the Ninth Heads of Government Conference in July 1974. The draft agreement, supported by most of the MDCs, had called for a policy of localization of the regional economy leading ultimately to the exclusion of foreign investment in some big areas of the economy (Payne 1980). The LDCs subsequently decided on forming the Eastern Caribbean Promotion Investment Service through which to attract foreign investment to their countries. The inability of member countries to reach a consensus on foreign investment goes beyond that of parochial concerns. It also reflects the lack of agreement on the meaning of development, and consequently the means to attain it, an issue which is fundamentally ideological (Demas 1974). This is exemplified by the responses to the Draft Agreement on Foreign Investment and the Development of Technology, which is based on a particular perspective of the role of foreign investment in development. Eckstein (1978) has suggested that the pursuit of different ideologies by CARICOM member countries has affected the philosophical and pragmatic bases for economic integration. However, it is perhaps more accurate to suggest that, because of the philosophical and pragmatic basis of CARICOM, it opens the way for the pursuit of different ideologies where each country is allowed to determine and pursue its own development strategy. Such a situation, quite often, not only leads to conflict at the level of policy formulation but, inevitably, makes the co-ordination of economic policy a difficult task. For instance, during the second half of the 1970s tensions grew within CARICOM because of the diverging development approaches adopted by countries such as Jamaica and Guyana on the one hand and Trinidad on the other. In a statement to parliament on 19 January 1977, Manley described his party's firm rejection of capitalism as the system upon which to base the future of Jamaica. According to him:

> capitalism necessarily involves the exploitation of the many in the interest of the few, and obliges individuals to pursue private gain at the expense of their fellow citizens without regard to the collective interests of the entire society (Eckstein 1978:13).

Jamaica's position, along with Guyana's, was to reject the role played by MNCs in the development of the region. At one May Day rally, President Forbes Burnham attacked the exploitative role played by the MNCs and stated that his government would not be buying any more soap produced by the MNCs in Trinidad (Eckstein 1978). Trinidad on the other hand saw her development as inextricably linked to MNCs. The government encouraged relations with them in areas such as oil, petro chemicals, finance, transport and agriculture. The Point Lisas industrialization plan relied substantially on the involvement of MNCs. Both Jamaica and Guyana, however, echoed their opposition to pursuing such diverse developmental strategies. Thus Eckstein states (1978:18) "it is obvious that this development must adversely affect growth in regional trade and in the process the entire integration movement".

The point being made here is that ideological consensus enhances the ability of the community to integrate economically. The Andean Pact, for instance, started out as an economic union with a common anti-imperialist policy, preferring instead to adopt strategies to protect members' national economies. It later experienced severe difficulties with formulation and implementation of policy because of Chilean fascism.

The pursuit of democratic socialism by Manley involved different policies from the brand of capitalism adopted by Williams. The former usually used fiscal and monetary policies directly to achieve egalitarianism and social justice; while the latter used these macro-economic tools of adjustment to stimulate industrial development with the expectation that jobs would result to alleviate unemployment. In fact, states Eckstein, these almost conflicting approaches to development do not allow for the "deepening of the economic union between such states, no freedom of movement of persons or capital can ever be possible, no harmonization of fiscal and monetary policies" (1978:19).

Even in the absence of such diverging ideological tendencies, as manifested in the 1980s, there is still some deepening of the integration process. For instance, one of the aims of economic policy co-ordination is the harmonization of fiscal incentives to industry, an objective of the Common Market since 1973. The scheme which recognizes the fact that economic and financial policies of member countries affect the economies of other member states has yet to be implemented (Payne 1980).

In addition, little progress has been made with the implementation of a Common External Tariff (CET) and the Common Protective Policy (CPP), the CET being part of the CARICOM Treaty since 1973. Aimed at protecting and developing the industrial base of the region, it was recognized by planners that the CET might sometimes work too slowly to prevent dislocation in local industries and that in CARICOM the level of CET was low compared to other Third World countries. Thus, the Common Protective Policy (CPP) or a regime of quantitative restrictions was added to the CET, the rationale being that it was more effective and easier to impose in the region. But, argues Payne, the provision made for the CPP is strikingly weak and undemanding since it virtually leaves it up to the member countries to implement as soon as they see fit — a distant prospect given the large differences in existing national quantitative restrictions systems". What therefore obtains in the light of this situation is that no mechanism exists for the prevention of unfair competition in industrial production given the differing policies of importation of raw materials required for manufacturing industries.

CARICOM planners have been unable to make any progress in the area of factor mobility (provided for in chapter 5 of the Annex). They hold the view that because of the nature of capital movements, free movement of capital and labour could lead to further polarization of development in the region. However, governments of the MDCs have categorically rejected the idea of free movement of labour as they argue that a massive influx of unskilled labour from the LDCs could aggravate the unemployment situation in their countries.

Another area in which the regional movement has been unable to make any substantial progress is that of production integration. This is concerned with the mechanisms for planning and integrating resource use so as to undertake joint production activities. Production integration really entails the pulling together in an organization of a number of processes undertaken jointly by member countries. However, with the exception of the Regional Food Plan, efforts at production integration have hardly gone beyond negotiated agreements (Payne 1980). In fact, some conflict has even resulted from efforts at production integration. Witness, for example, the ill-fated aluminium smelter project between Guyana, Jamaica and Trinidad which had been proposed for 1971. Jamaica, Guyana and Trinidad were supposed to hold equity shares of 33 per cent, 33 per cent and 34 per cent respectively. The aluminium smelter was to be established in Trinidad, which would provide the natural gas for its operation. Another smelter was also to be built in Guyana utilizing hydro-electricity. The equity shares on this project were distributed among Guyana (52 per cent), Jamaica (24 per cent) and Trinidad (24 per cent). However, the project never got off the ground due to a conflict which developed between Manley and Williams, concerning Jamaica's decision to supply bauxite to Venezuela. According to Williams, the decision by Jamaica to enter into a bauxite agreement with Venezuela was tantamount to an attack on the CARICOM scheme. Williams was of the view that the planned increase in the export of aluminium by Venezuela, partly supported by the Jamaican bauxite, would have an effect on the viability of the CARICOM project, a view which Manley did not share. An additional factor which seemed to compound the situation was that there seemed to be no consultation on the issue before the agreement was undertaken (Payne 1980).

The inability of the integration movement to harmonize fiscal incentives to industry, to implement the CET and CPP, to allow for the free movement of capital and labour, and to engage in production integration are clear indicators that the Common Market has failed to live up to its objectives. Indeed, such a failure simply underscores the weakness of the concept and operation of CARICOM. In each case, individual national interests, most vividly exemplified by the Manley-Williams controversy, have inhibited the proper formulation and adoption of policies which could work positively for the region as a whole.

Regional Integration and Functional Co-operation

Although functional co-operation is the most successful area of regional integration, it has failed to live up to the stated aims of the Treaty. Functional co-operation, which pre-dates CARICOM, going back to the days of the Federation, has expanded over the years and, according to Payne, the programme has made significant contributions to the quality of life of the people of the region. However, the full realization of the potential of such co-operation remains subdued because of the perpetual individualist attitude that has come to characterize the movement. Divisiveness has also been encouraged by the misguided idea of separating economic integration from the other two major objectives. In this regard, four areas of functional co-operation spring immediately to mind: air transport; travel within the region; harmonization of the law and legal systems of member states; and, last but not least, culture.

These four areas of functional co-operation stand out for two basic reasons. First, it is in these areas that there has been least co-operation (Payne 1980). Secondly, it is fundamentally through achievements in these four areas that the aims of the Treaty — the efficient operation of certain common services and activities, along with the development of greater understanding among peoples of the Community and the advancement of cultural development — are realized. Incidentally, Demas (1974) has also acknowledged that co-operation in these areas is vital to the deepening of the integration process.

In spite of the potential benefits to be derived from co-operation in air transport, the region has made little progress in this area outside joint representation at the International Civil Aviation Organization (Payne 1980). Steve DeCastro, in a study of air transport in the region (1967), has recommended the setting up of a regional airline which would work to save unnecessary duplication of air travel facilities and airlines. The inability of member countries to pursue such a policy has led Demas to conclude (1974:71):

> the countries of the region have not yet recognized that this is one central area where they have to pool their bargaining power and regulate the operations of a foreign air carrier in the *interest of the region* (writer's emphasis).

Demas is indeed asking much, given the nature of the Treaty which in no way commits member countries to such a policy in the interest of the region. Thus, in the absence of such a spirit of regionalism, member countries have established a proliferation of airlines, sometimes duplicating air routes as in the case of Guyana Airways and British West Indian Airways (BWIA). Even the LDCs (those least able to afford such a venture) have established national airlines. Among them are Saint Lucia Airlines and recently, the American dominated Grenada Airlines. This situation is by no means accidental for, as the Leeward Islands Air Travel (LIAT) affair has demonstrated, regional governments have always tended to pursue policies in fulfilment of their own interests.

When in 1974 the British firm which owned the small LIAT went into liquidation, regional governments found extreme difficulty in reaching a consensus on the issue of joint ownership (Payne 1980). This was even in view of the fact that LIAT was the only air link between most of the territories comprising the LDCs. In the end, all agreed to the plan, except Trinidad which offered instead to provide a soft loan equal to its proposed equity share. The Trinidad position was based on the fact that it already had a commitment to BWIA which was a rather burdensome undertaking.

Subsequently, Trinidad changed its position and agreed to the original plan of purchasing shares in LIAT.

The implications of this scenario for greater integration in the field of air travel are certainly not encouraging. The inability of BWIA to secure the task of being the official regional air carrier is further confirmation of this view. Indeed, only Barbados has responded positively to Trinidad's bid to use BWIA. as the regional air carrier. It is important, however, to note that this decision came in 1986 after the government of Barbados decided to divest its national airline, Caribbean Airways, because of financial losses.

Progress in the area of intra-regional travel has also been less than encouraging. At the Ninth Heads of Government Meeting in July 1984, some countries took steps agreeing to allow nationals of member countries to travel on a common travel document. However, such a policy is yet to be implemented (Payne 1980). At the present moment intra-regional travel is characterized by much "red tape" and forbidding immigration laws. These laws make it easier for American citizens than people from the region to enter most of the Caribbean countries. In fact, in the past, some governments have gone as far as requesting visas from nationals of some countries — Grenadians, for example, once needed visas to enter Jamaica.

The fact that little progress has been made in the area of regional travel has serious implications for factor mobility since the tender of services and free movement of capital require unrestricted intra-regional travel. Indeed, one of the problems of the Treaty is that by dividing factor mobility and regional travel into separate "treaties", consistency is not maintained, as all member countries do not give equal priority to both the Common Market and functional co-operation.

A similar situation applies to the harmonization of law and legal systems. The harmonization of fiscal incentives to industry and the avoidance of double taxation pre-supposes the harmonization of law. Although formal steps have been made to harmonize fiscal incentives and the avoidance of double taxation, the lack of synchronization in law combined with the individualist policies of member countries continues to frustrate the realization of its objectives (Demas 1974; Hippolyte-Manigat 1979). Because of the continuous problem of lack of implementation by member countries, the scheme is still being reviewed after a decision taken by the Heads of Government in 1986.

However, CARICOM has recorded absolutely no progress in the harmonization of legal systems. No development, for instance, has been made since the 1970 proposal for the establishment of a Commonwealth Caribbean Court of Appeal to replace the Judicial Committee of the Privy

Council. Demas suggests that this is due to a lack of self-confidence which characterizes the West Indian psyche, while Payne (1980) contends that apart from financial reasons pertaining to the funding of such an institution, some member countries are unwilling to sever ties with the "Mother Country". While it is difficult to arbitrate between these two competing view points, opinions are divided on the questions of the ability and parameters of a regional legal system.

Finally, one more area in which little or no progress has been made is that of cultural development — recognized since 1972 at the Seventh Heads of Government Conference as an important vehicle in the process towards greater regional unity (Payne 1980). To this end, a cultural officer was appointed to the Secretariat to work in the promotion of cultural activities in the region. Nevertheless, except for the Caribbean Festival of Creative Arts (CARIFESTA), which is a cultural extravanganza of countries in and outside of CARICOM, there are no other organized cultural events in the region. Even the staging of CARIFESTA has encountered its problems. Staged only four times since its inception in 1972, regional governments have begun to to complain that this festival is too expensive to be hosted by a single country. Jamaica, for example, did not host the proposed 1988 CARIFESTA because of economic difficulties. The last minute decision to announce its position on the event — just six months before the festival — is a clear reflection of the scant importance paid by that country to the role of culture in integration. This probably reflects, generally, the attitude of most of the other member countries, since regional governments can point to few other areas of cultural co-operation besides CARIFESTA.

Even if regional leaders are unwilling as a group to engage in the integration of culture, some of them are certainly not unaware of its possible role in the deepening of the integration process. Erskine Sandiford, prime minister of Barbados, giving a speech in honour of the president of Venezuela, Dr. Jaime Lusinchi on 15 July 1987 said:

> I believe that if one is seeking to understand and appreciate a country's foreign policy and posture, one must first seek to understand that country's culture. For values which shape the lives of people living in communities tend eventually to inform their behaviour, both in internal and external relationships with neighbours (Sandiford 1988:5).

Maurice Bishop, the late prime minister of Grenada, also acknowledged the role of culture in fostering greater regional unity. He even suggested the decentralization and scaling down of CARIFESTA to make it more manageable for regional governments to host (Kinshasa 1984). This suggestion was totally ignored, in spite of the impending problems involving cost and administration of this event.

Why have regional governments continued to ignore cultural development in light of its recognized role in the integration process? The answer, according to Bishop, is clear — CARICOM countries are engaged in serving individual interests as well as making profits for MNCs (Kinshasa 1984).

Regional Integration and the Co-ordination of Foreign Policy

The co-ordination of foreign policy is one of the most ambitious, but also most controversial and problematical areas of regional integration. Admittedly, being unique among other regional movements in its decision to co-ordinate foreign policy, CARICOM has made some important successes in this area. For example, the solidarity shown in the Belize-Guatemala dispute and the success in obtaining agreement on a protocol to amend the Organization of American States Charter to permit Guyana and Belize to enter the Organization by 1990, testify to such achievements.

Article 17 (of the main section) of the Treaty provides for general foreign policy co-ordination. The Article allows for a Standing Committee of Ministers responsible for foreign affairs. It makes recommendations to the governments of the member states with a view to realizing "the fullest possible co-ordination of foreign policies within their respective competences".

Article 34 of the Common Market Annex includes the provision that member countries "shall seek" progressive co-ordination of their trade relations with third countries or a group of third countries. The Article also requires them to transmit to the Secretariat particulars of any trade or aid agreement entered into.

The Group of Experts Report, recognizing the shortcomings of co-operation in the area of foreign policy co-ordination, made recommendations that the territories of the region intensify efforts to achieve a greater degree of co-ordination in their foreign policies (*The Caribbean Community in the 1980s*) Lloyd Seawar has also noted that:

> while there have been some notable achievements through co-ordination, there have also been crucial areas in which, although it would have appeared that co-ordinated action should have been the imperative, individual states have steadily eschewed the group approach, preferring instead to go it alone" (Seawar 1988:62).

Such a perspective can be used to explain Jamaica's decision to enter into the bauxite agreement with Venezuela without consultation and in light of previously made plans to be involved in the aluminium smelter project with Guyana and Trinidad. A further tendency towards bilateralism in Jamaica's foreign policy was reflected in the decision also to include Mexico as shareholder in the new Jamaican aluminium plant. The Mexican government had in 1974 signed an agreement with CARICOM, as a group, on trade and co-operation (Payne 1980).

Arising out of Jamaica's action was a dispute between Williams and Manley, in the context of which Williams not only castigated Manley but also implicated Venezuela's motives as an attempt to recolonize the region. Williams even made a speech to his party, the People's National Movement (PNM), later published under the title *The Threat to the Caribbean Community,* in which he attacked Venezuela's perceived territorial ambitions in the region and bitterly denounced Jamaica's decision to embark on an agreement with Venezuela. Manley, however, was firm in his disagreement with Williams over the recolonization thesis, suggesting instead that the project was simply a co-operative effort with a sister Caribbean country (Payne 1980).

This dispute brings to the fore an important issue yet unresolved by CARICOM — conflicting perceptions of the concept of the Caribbean. Payne (1980) identifies the two basic perceptions as the "Williams Latin American Doctrine" and the "Manley Latin American Doctrine". The former treats the motives behind certain Latin American states' relationships with CARICOM countries with great caution and suspicion. The tendency here is towards discouraging relations with Latin American states. The Caribbean is therefore defined to exclude Central and Latin American states, save what were once the three Guianas. On the other hand, the Manley doctrine seeks to promote closer ties and co-operation with Latin American states, with a view to creating a new world economic order. The Caribbean is therefore defined as constituting both the Commonwealth and Latin American states. It is not clear which of these perspectives holds greatest support within the regional movement. However, the fact that Jamaica got the support of most of the member countries during the dispute is some indication that some Latin American countries, such as Venezuela, may be looked upon as close friends.

The conflict over the co-ordination of foreign policy is also the result of divergent views of regional development and the role of the Caribbean in international politics. The Caribbean Democratic Union, which comprises regional politicians of "like mind" who perceive the interests of the region as closely tied with those of the United States of America, represents one side of the development spectrum. On the other hand, there are those governments which believe in a non-aligned policy where regional self-reliance and sovereignty are fundamental aspects of development. The socialist regimes of Manley and Burnham along with the administration of the late Errol Barrow (and now Erksine Sandiford) support such an approach. These different perspectives were clearly manifested during the Grenada crisis.

After the overthrow of the Maurice Bishop regime in Grenada in October 1983, CARICOM governments met to decide on a course of action. There were two meetings, the first was not attended by Trinidad, while Barbados missed the second. The first was held in Barbados, and the second in Trinidad. However, during the first meeting, Barbados, Jamaica and the OECS took action to allow the United States of America to intervene in the region (Anderson 1988). The Trinidad prime minister went to the second meeting with a view to taking action, when in fact action had already been taken. Such an act was in breach of the spirit of the Treaty, which calls for regional consensus before action is taken on such delicate issues. Guyana, incidentally, had objected to the agreement at the first meeting. In addition, opposition parties in Saint Lucia, Saint Vincent, Guyana, Trinidad and Barbados condemned the decision to sanction United States intervention in Grenada.

That a regional leader, Eugenia Charles, made a visit to Jamaica to discuss the issue with the then United States Secretary of State, George Bush, without regional consensus, not only points to an unwillingness to exhaust collective efforts, but indicates the acceptance by some regional leaders of a particular role for the United States of America in the region. Additionally, according to the late Errol Barrow, the decision was clearly one of "invoking an unregistered treaty of mutual assistance to carry out precisely what the treaty was designed to protect against" (*Caribbean Contact* 1985:13).

That some regional leaders were opposed to such a policy is indicative of another perspective with regard to United States involvement in the region, hence by implication, a different view of regionalism, exemplified in a statement by Errol Barrow, viz.

> it would take a master with the stature of Sophocles to properly dramatise the tragedy to the people of Grenada or to illustrate the inevitable damage to Caribbean sovereignty and self-respect, not to speak of the systematic dismantling of the Caribbean Community (*Caribbean Contact* 1985:13).

Further evidence of conflict over foreign policy co-ordination due to diverging perspectives of the role of the region in the international arena is reflected in the difficulty of arriving at a consensus on Haiti. After the toppling of President Leslie Manigat of Haiti, Lester Bird, spokesman for the Heads of Government meeting on Haiti (held on 5 July 1988), said "the heads have not agreed upon what the signal should be. There are different emphases by different heads" (*Caribbean Contact* 1985:1).

He further admitted that sharp differences existed on the matter. There has also been controversy over policies on the Southern Africa struggle. In 1976 a special meeting called principally to discuss matters pertaining to the University of the West Indies, ended in disarray when Jamaica and Guyana decided not to discuss the issue of aid to Mozambique, which had just closed its border to Rhodesia (now Zimbabwe), as a separate issue from sporting links with South Africa. At this time, both Guyana and Jamaica had attained high profile roles in the Non-Aligned Movement, openly voicing support for liberation movements the world over (Payne 1980). Trinidad disagreed with such a position, suggesting instead that they preferred to wait until the United Nations considered the matter. Both Trinidad and Barbados also refused to grant Cuban troops en route to Angola permission to use their airports to refuel Cuban planes. While both Barbados and Trinidad based their positions on neutrality amongst the fighting factions, Guyana and Jamaica openly gave support to the revolutionary governments of both Mozambique and Angola (Payne 1980).

Sectional Interests and Regional Integration

Although much of the foregoing discussion has showed a major weakness of CARICOM as emanating from the overriding concerns with national interests, it is also true that another shortcoming of the movement is that its conceptual framework has made it into an elitist institution which is, fundamentally, concerned with fulfilling sectional interests at the expense of larger regional objectives.

The elitist nature of CARICOM is clearly the result of its neo-functionalist origins which have led to the establishment of supra-national institutions to co-ordinate regional policies. The issue of integration is consequently the exclusive preserve of technocrats, bureaucrats, politicians and business people. Regional integration has, therefore, come to be regarded as a technical and administrative matter. It is not surprising, then, that many writers have decried this approach to integration, suggesting instead the need for the masses to be engaged in the process. William Demas, one of the architects of the integration movement, has admitted that the lack of people's involvement in CARICOM can work to the detriment of regional integration. He states:

> Governments of the region have not yet found a satisfactory solution at the national level to the critical problem to two-way communication between governments and the people. If this is true at the national level, it will be all the more true as regards communication at the regional level in so far as [the] aims, objectives and nature of CARICOM are concerned (Demas 1974:72).

Wendell Samuel has also argued that one of the reasons why governments have difficulty in implementing policies decided upon at the CARICOM level stems from the lack of mass support for them. Accordingly, he advises that "all efforts to move forward will be to no avail if integration remains an activity confined to government ministries and a few influential members of the business community" (Samuel 1987:20).

Perhaps the most important elite group served by the regional movement is from the business community. The fact that the region is comprised of developing capitalist countries which subscribe to the idea of free trade, as advocated by CARICOM, suggests that economic integration is ultimately concerned with private commercial interests. But with the predominance of MNCs in most Caribbean territories, economic integration inevitably leads to the reinforcement of American hegemony in the region and the pursuit of interests contrary to the aims of the integration objective. Thus, Thomas writes:

> Shell or Esso with different facilities on different islands would not be rational in the pursuit of their shareholders' interests, if they were to act as if each island is truly an island unto itself. As would be expected they routinely make integrated decisions based on their regional interests; which is, to secure the profitable exploitation of regional resources at their command (Thomas 1979:287).

Meanwhile, the interests of these MNCs remain protected as the member countries are still unable, after more than a decade, to arrive at a consensus on foreign investment. In addition, Schedule II (Appendix of the Treaty) which gives a list of products that are always to be treated as having been produced in the region, whether or not this is the case, only serves to confirm CARICOM's desire to protect MNCs.

The ability of the Trinidad Manufacturers' Association to convince its government, in 1986, to take measures to protect that country's garment industry, and the pressure exerted by the JMA, which caused the Jamaican government in 1975 to take action against countries which were in breach of the trade agreement, are vivid indicators of the important role of private capital in the regional movement. It is worthy of note that in both cases the actions of the manufacturers' associations resulted from the fact that their particular interests were being undermined.

Conclusions

This chapter has attempted to demonstrate that CARICOM is weak and unstable. With regards to the major objectives of the movement, the discussion has shown: first, that the pursuit of insular national interests has undermined the realization of wider regional goals. This is perhaps the most crucial with respect to economic integration. When crises within the world economy have occurred, member states, instead of acting in solidarity in the common interest, have continuously sought to unilaterally protect their national economies. A reason for this situation is the way in which these countries have been integrated into the world economy. Indeed, one of the shortcomings of CARICOM is that it has not sought to change the existing development strategy. In fact, the flexible and pragmatic nature of CARICOM has opened up the door for member countries to pursue different development strategies on their own, without consultation and co-ordination. The result has been conflict with regard to policy formulation and implementation in all three areas of co-operation. Secondly, the structure of CARICOM is elitist and is also designed to serve sectional interests at the expense of mass involvement. This has also prevented CARICOM from achieving a genuinely integrated region.

The discussion has sought to attribute the weakness of the integration movement primarily to the conceptualization of CARICOM. The Caribbean Community is guided by a treaty which heralds economic pragmatism in anticipation of the convergence of national interests into wider regional ones. The reality has not been encouraging. It is clear that if the regional movement is to forge ahead, another approach which places regional interests above national and sectional ones has to be pursued. Such an approach must seek a clear definition of development and eschew pragmatic and conflicting individual interests. Such an approach would therefore require a system of ideas which would acknowledge the intimacy of national and regional development and would guide the formulation and implementation of policies to such an end. In the words of Hippolyte-Manigat:

> for the strengthening of an integration movement the regional perspective should, whatever the circumstances, prevail over the national horizons and no individual initiative, however justifiable in the name of national interests, should impede collective policies (Hippolyte-Manigat 1979:40).

This approach is one which is based on an ideology of regionalism. It is the lack of such an ideology within CARICOM which has robbed the regional movement of stability and strength. Chapter 4 has attempted to show, empirically, that an ideology of regionalism does not exist within the region.

CHAPTER 5

Attitudes Towards Integration:
Ideology or Ideation?

In this chapter it is argued that there is no ideology of regionalism among the elites of both Jamaica and Saint Lucia. The argument is posited on the strength of evidence from an analysis of the data arising from a survey of elite attitudes towards integration. The survey was conducted in Jamaica and Saint Lucia.

The analysis of the data revealed that the respondents do not have a coherent and organized body of perceptions and explanations about the region which would serve to direct action, through policy or otherwise, to strengthen regionalism. However, the data show that a weak and diffused regionalist sentiment is shared by respondents of the two countries. This sentiment is the product of regionalist ideation or the formation and development of ideas and mental images about the region. This regionalist ideation is stronger among the Saint Lucian respondents as a group but for both countries it is weakest among the economic elite.

In order to demonstrate the above claim, the discussion is confined to the examination of the extent to which respondents' attitudes comprise elements of an ideology of regionalism. The discussion is thus structured so that it revolves around the extent to which there exists a coherent and organized set of attitudes in relation to:

1. beliefs, or how elites perceive the region;

2. explanations for the present condition of the regional movement;

3. actions to counter the fragility of regionalism.

An attempt will also be made to account for the variations in the degree and nature of the regionalist orientation between the two countries and elite groups. Finally, the discussion yields a number of observations.

It should be noted that the discussion draws considerably on secondary sources in order to highlight and reinforce various inferences drawn from the data. Also, as the survey did not utilize a scientific sample, the use of secondary data assumes a complementary role. Finally, the integration of secondary information has also led to greater concretization of seemingly abstract sentiments expressed by respondents.

Perception of the Region

The question of identity has constantly occupied centre stage for writers on Caribbean integration. Demas, for example, argues that there is a single Caribbean identity which sets the basis for political integration (Demas 1974). On the other hand, Colin Clarke contends that there are a number of identities within the region which are oftentimes conflicting, preventing closer regional integration (Clarke 1984). Interestingly, the data support both claims, although there seems to be greater support for Clarke's argument. For instance, although the overwhelming majority of respondents from both Saint Lucia and Jamaica agree that there is a Caribbean identity (Table 5.1), there is less agreement in relation to the characteristics of this identity (Table 5.2).

Table 5.1: Existence of a Caribbean Identity (Responses by Country)

Country	Number responding	Per cent "yes"
Jamaica (n=100)	100	79.0
Saint Lucia (n=82)	82	81.4

Table 5.2: Main Characteristics of a Caribbean Identity
(% Response by Country)

Characteristics	Jamaica (n=100)	Saint Lucia (n=82)
Common culture	55.0	55.7
Geographical location	18.0	37.8
Common history	36.0	50.0
Common social, political and economic features	24.0	31.7
External perception	14.0	4.9

Since a large number of respondents agreed that a Caribbean identity exists, and there is some degree of agreement regarding the content of such an identity, one may be led to conclude that this indicates the existence of some form of a Caribbean identity albeit a rather diffused one. It is, however, clear that there is an overwhelming commitment to separate national identities. The comparatively larger degree of cohesion in perception within each country suggests that strong national identities co-exist with a weak Caribbean identity.

An examination of the data shows that there are five characteristics of this identity with the greatest degree of support for common culture. The support for common history and geographical location plays a much more significant role for Saint Lucian respondents. External perception or how the region is seen from the outside is evidently much more important for Jamaicans than for Saint Lucians. An additional difference between the two countries relates to the fact that Jamaicans were more abstract and vague, especially in referring to the cultural and historical aspects of identity. Specificity occurred when reference was made to cricket and the external perception of the region. Interestingly, many of the Jamaican respondents were of the view that the Jamaican identity was the most dominant in the region. They were of the opinion that outside of the region, particularly in England and the United States, West Indians were seen as Jamaicans. These views are seen in typical comments made by some Jamaican respondents (see Appendix IX for respondent key).

"The identity comes when you are abroad, how people perceive you and how you are perceived." (01)

"Outside of the region all West Indians are seen as Jamaicans." (02)

"I would say to some extent there is a Caribbean identity. This is seen through cricket, you know when we play cricket we are all West Indians." (03)

Saint Lucians, on the other hand, tended to see identity in terms of language, common ethnic groups, colonial experiences, music, cricket and carnival. Few referred to external perceptions and there was no mention of being subsumed under any particular country's identity, although there was reference to the strong influence of Rastafarianism and reggae music of Jamaica in the region. Witness, for example, some opinions which were commonly expressed:

"I think one can say as West Indians we share common life styles and ideals. This is seen in our music and in our culture - carnival, calypso and so on." (04)

"Before slavery there were no such people as Caribbean people. Our history which is a mixture of European and African cultures is unique to us sociologically and historically; we have a common identity which is West Indian." (05)

"Without a doubt there is a Caribbean identity. Our history, our culture, reggae, calypso and carnival are powerful manifestations of this." (06)

The difference in perception between these two countries can be seen within the context of a socio-political situation where Saint Lucians have had closer contact with people from other Eastern Caribbean countries through political unions (for example, the Federation of the Leeward and Windward Islands of 1871 and the West Indies Federation), and migration. After the demise of the West Indies Federation in 1962, Saint Lucians got together with the other lesser developed countries of the Eastern Caribbean to form Associated Statehood. Even after receiving independence, these countries have continued to have close institutional contact through the Organization of Eastern Caribbean States (OECS). Saint Lucians have also engaged in a considerable amount of intra-regional migration, making them both importers and exporters of migrants from most of the territories in the region (Wiltshire-Brodber 1984).

On the other hand, Jamaicans have, historically, had little contact with the people of the Eastern Caribbean. In fact, it has been argued that one of the major obstacles which faced the West Indies Federation was the isolation of Jamaica from the rest of the Caribbean. This comparatively weak link with the Eastern Caribbean was partly responsible for Norman

Manley's decision to prefer a weak federal structure to a strongly centralized one as advocated by Eric Williams. Small wonder why, therefore, Lewis argued that after the secession of Jamaica, had common sense prevailed, the Eastern Caribbean leaders would have seized the opportunity to build a strongly centralized federation (W.A. Lewis 1965).

Even though communication between Jamaica and the rest of the region has seen tremendous improvement, comparatively speaking, there is still little interaction except through the University of the West Indies and sports. The greatest degree of interaction probably occurs in the large West Indian emigrant communities in Canada, the United Kingdom and the United States of America, which have been dominated by Jamaicans.

The perception of a dominant Jamaican identity shared by some respondents may reflect how some Jamaicans view themselves in relation to the rest of the region. Being the largest country in terms of population and possessing an enviable reputation for sports and music internationally, Jamaicans evidently have independent bases for seeing themselves as part of the international system. For the Caribbean countries, success in sports and music have been the most important ways of achieving international recognition in a world where they possess little economic, military or political power. For example, cricket is not only an important unifying force in the region, it is also an expression of regional prowess against larger and stronger countries, especially the former colon-izer, England. Jamaica's almost Herculean success in international sports, and its gift to the world of superstars such as Bob Marley and Jimmy Cliff, have clearly made it stand out among the countries of the Third World. Additionally, Jamaica's influence in CARICOM seems to be of great significance because of the comparatively larger population size which makes it, technically, the single largest market for regionally made commodities. Thus, it is not unreasonable to argue that Jamaicans may have a tendency to see themselves as the "elite" of the region. It is this "superior" attitude which may have been an underlying factor in Prime Minister Seaga's statements to the effect that Jamaica was not interested in political integration with the rest of the region, given that the Federation had failed, because of "…. the great difference in size and levels of development among the countries" *(Caribbean Contact 1985:1)*.

This point is further illustrated in the comments of just under one-half of the Jamaican respondents who, when asked where in the Caribbean they would prefer to live, gave responses which were typical of the following:

> "I don't know if I would live in any of the other Eastern Caribbean countries because of a lack of opportunities and lower levels of development." (07)

"Probably the only countries I could think about are Barbados and Trinidad. The others have little to offer in terms of career development. I would not want to choose a country that is not as developed as Jamaica." (08)

Important differences in perception of identity also exist at the elite and age group levels. In relation to perceptions between elite groups, the data show that there exists a difference in perception of the region between the economic elite on the one hand and the cultural and political groups on the other. In both countries, the cultural and political elite distinguished the region most often in terms of its culture and history; the economic elite less so, placing greater emphasis on the economic aspects. The following two comments from members of the economic elite and cultural elite, respectively, highlight these two basic emphases:

"I believe that there is a Caribbean identity in the attitudes and otherwise. However, the Caribbean must see themselves as one unit or market, the way the Europeans had to over the years ... Strength will not come until the politicians can get past ideological splits and come to an understanding about exports and common currencies and the part they play." (09)

"There is a Caribbean identity. Take for example, say, Viv Richards — there is nobody in the region who doesn't know who Viv is. Take calypso — if a Caribbean person does not know what that represents, then that is not a Caribbean person." (10)

It is this concern with economic issues by the economic elite which appears to account for the comparatively low percentage "yes" response to identity. That is to say, views regarding identity appeared to be based on their experiences within CARICOM. Many of these experiences were negative, especially among the Saint Lucian respondents. These negative experiences perhaps explain why the Saint Lucian economic elite have, overall, the lowest positive response to the existence of a Caribbean identity (Table 5.3). Views such as the following were often expressed by members of the Saint Lucian economic elite:

"I think that the concept of CARICOM is good. I don't think that it has worked as effectively as people thought it would." (11)

"One major problem of CARICOM is the fact that there is no real free trade among the countries. Every country wants to protect its own economy. We have been having difficulty in exporting to some of the markets of the so-called MDCs. Governments just aren't sticking to the rules." (12)

Table 5.3: Existence of a Caribbean Identity
(% Response by Elite Group)

Elite group	Yes		No	
	Jamaica (n=100)	Saint Lucia (n=82)	Jamaica (n=100)	Saint Lucia (n=82)
Economic	68.4	50.0	13.1	41.6
Cultural	90.6	93.5	-	3.2
Political	80.0	100	13.3	-

It is the case that the Lesser Developed Countries (LDCs) have, traditionally, been unable to reap as many economic benefits from CARICOM as the More Developed Countries (MDCs) (see chapter 4). In addition, conflicts within CARICOM resulting from the MDCs' desire to protect their faltering economies, have resulted in tensions within the region. It was partly for that reason the Organization of Eastern Caribbean States (OECS) was founded in 1981. Vaughan Lewis, Secretary General of the OECS, in explaining the reasons for the evolution of this organization, states:

> The initial optimism which had marked the founding of the Caribbean Community in 1973 had largely disappeared under the weight of regional economic difficulties, particularly the trade restrictions which some of the large CARICOM countries were forced to adopt as their domestic economies experienced severe difficulties. In an atmosphere of regional self protection and protectionism and the weakening of major markets for manufacturers from the lesser developed countries of CARICOM there had developed a clear need for the LDCs to take action to defend themselves (Lewis 1987:5).

It has been argued that a factor which contributes to the weak regional identity relates to the negative way in which people perceive the region (Clarke 1984). According to Demas, what the region lacks is "the kind of identity that goes with self-confidence; the kind of identity that generates a feeling of self-respect, self-worth and more dignity on the part of the people" (Demas 1974:3). This negative perception has led Demas further to conclude that Caribbean people are lacking in consciousness of their true interests and true potential, leading them to become, as V.S. Naipaul would have it, "mimic men". In one of his most sagacious, illuminating and highly entertaining prose pieces, *The Mimic Men*, Naipual engages in a discussion of the colonized mentality of the West Indian, who uncritically mimics the culture of the former colonial rulers. Such negative attitudes seem to be reflected in the data. When asked if it was normal for them to purchase commodities made in the region, the overwhelming majority of responses in both countries was negative (Table 5.4).

**Table 5.4: Preferences for the Purchase of
Regionally Made Commodities
(% Responses in Both Countries)**

Preferences	Jamaica	Saint Lucia
No	66.0	68.3
Yes	28.0	22.0
No response	6.0	9.8
Totals	100	100
	n=100	n=82

Except for respondents of the economic elite and those in the 35-45 age group who show comparatively marginally highest negative response, no significant variations existed between elite or age groups (Tables 5.5, 5.6, 5.7).

These results, overall, may be seen as an indicator of a negative regionalist orientation among most of the respondents. However, two factors should be considered in making this point. First, almost all of the respondents who gave a negative reply stated that their choice of commodity was a function of price and commodity. Their decision not to purchase commodities made in the region was often the result of dissatisfaction with commodities which were previously bought. Hence, these negative experiences tended to condition expectations which often inhibited the purchase of regionally made goods. Therefore, a simple "yes" or "no" answer may not be an adequate indicator of integration sentiment.

On the other hand, the choice of a commodity might also have been the result of socialized preferences as people's perception of quality is often

Table 5.5: Preferences for the Purchase of Regionally Made Commodities (by Group Type)

Preferences	Jamaica		
	Economic	Political	Cultural
No	65.8	65.6	66.7
Yes	23.7	34.4	26.7
No response	10.5	-	6.6
Totals	100	100	100
	n=38	n=32	n=30

Table 5.6: Preferences for the Purchase of Regionally Made Commodities (by Group Type)

Preferences	Saint Lucia		
	Economic	Political	Cultural
No	83.4	61.3	61.6
Yes	8.3	35.5	19.2
No response	8.3	3.2	19.2
Totals	100	100	100
	n=24	n=31	n=26

Table 5.7: Preferences for the Purchase of Regionally Made Commodities (by Age Group)

Preferences	Jamaica and Saint Lucia			
	18-25	26-35	36-45	46+
No	66.7	59.3	75.7	58.1
Yes	33.3	35.6	15.7	29.0
No Response	-	5.1	8.6	12.9
Totals	100	100	100	100
	n=9	n=59	n=70	n=31

influenced by advertising and packaging. Communications analysts have argued that the media in the region play an important role in shaping values and preferences (Brown and Sanatan 1987). Given the influence of the media in the region, with their sophisticated techniques of advertising especially in relation to foreign made products, it is not unreasonable to expect people to prefer foreign made commodities. An additional factor worth considering is the view that, historically, people of the region have tended to prefer foreign made commodities (Beckford 1972). Such an attitude seems to be a legacy of colonialism where people were socialized to see the region as inferior to the "mother country" and other European nations (G. Lewis 1968). It is therefore understandable when garment manufacturers of the region attach foreign labels to their products in order to boost sales among the local population. The high percentage of "no" responses may therefore be indicative of this historically derived negative perception of the region.

Secondly, respondents interpreted "Caribbean made" commodities to also include commodities made in their respective countries. In the light of earlier conclusions which point to a tendency among Jamaicans to equate being West Indian with being Jamaican, the comparatively higher positive responses among them may be seen as a reflection of nationalist rather than regionalist sentiment. (This is not to suggest that there is necessarily always an inverse relationship between attitudes towards nationalism and region-alism.) The comparatively lower positive responses among the older age groups and the economic elite may therefore be seen as an expression of different levels of nationalism.

A further manifestation of the lack of regional consciousness can be inferred from the data. For example, each respondent was asked whether he/she would accept as a member of parliament and as prime minister of the country, someone born in another Caribbean country. The overwhelming majority of respondents from both countries replied in the affirmative (Tables 5.8, 5.9).

More Jamaican respondents seemed willing to accept "outsiders" both as members of parliament and as prime minister. Nevertheless, in both cases respondents seemed less in favour of an immigrant becoming prime minister. This is probably because such a position is at the pinnacle of public office and therefore requires someone who identifies closely with the aspirations of the people. Such sentiment is likely to be more associated with someone born in the country.

However, although the question was posed with respect to the region, the response should be treated quite cautiously. Of central importance is that

**Table 5.8: Acceptability of Naturalized Citizens as
Prime Minister and Member of Parliament
(% response)**

Response	Jamaica n=100	Saint Lucia n=82
Prime Minister		
No	9.0	12.2
Yes	80.0	73.2
Not sure	7.0	9.8
No response	4.0	4.8
Totals	100	100
Member of Parliament		
No	4.0	7.3
Yes	90.0	84.1
Not sure	-	3.7
No response	6.0	4.9
Totals	100	100

the majority of the respondents from both countries felt that their answers would have remained the same for persons outside of the region. In other words, the fact that the persons came from the region bore no particular significance to the response. Such an attitude, by implication, does not indicate any perception of a common identification with the peoples of the region but equates the region with extra-regional countries. According to this popular response: "It does not matter where the person is from, as long as he is accepted by the people". (13)

Further testimony to this weak regional consciousness, albeit to a lesser degree, is manifested in the responses to the question of where respondents preferred to have their children receive their tertiary education (Table 5.9).

It is indeed significant that, despite the majority preference for regional education, about one-third of the respondents from each country preferred extra-regional education. This extra-regional preference was

Table 5.9: Place Preferred for Tertiary Education for Children
(% Response)

Where preferred	Jamaica n = 100	Saint Lucia n = 82
Region	56.0	67.1
Extra-region	14.0	14.6
No preference	27.0	17.1
No response	3.0	1.2
Totals	100	100

clearly more significant for the economic elite and those in the 26-35 and 36-45 age groups (Tables 5.10, 5.11, 5.12). The responses for extra-regional education were fairly evenly distributed between the United Kingdom, the United States of America and Canada for respondents from both countries.

Table 5.10: Place Preferred for Tertiary Education for Children
(% Response by Group Type)

	Jamaica		
Where Preferred	Economic	Political	Cultural
Region	47.4	59.4	63.3
Extra-region	23.7	9.4	10.0
No preference	28.9	31.2	26.7
Totals	100	100	100
	n=38	n=32	n=30

However, how does one reconcile the argument of negative perception of the region with the majority preference for regional education? There are two likely explanations for this phenomenon. The great preference for regional education might be a reflection of a high degree of regional consciousness and commitment to regionalism. On the other hand, respondents could well be echoing views that are now current among the contemporary intelligentsia while disguising their real opinions. This latter explanation appears to be more plausible. What makes it a more realistic

Table 5.11: Place Preferred for Tertiary Education for Children
(% Response by Group Type)

	Saint Lucia		
Where Preferred	**Economic**	**Political**	**Cultural**
Region	45.8	77.4	73.1
Extra-region	33.3	6.5	7.7
No preference	20.9	16.1	19.2
Totals	100	100	100
	n=24	n=31	n=26

Table 5.12: Place Preferred for Tertiary Education for Children
(% Response by Age Group)

	Jamaica and Saint Lucia			
	Age Group			
Where preferred	**18-25**	**26-35**	**36-45**	**46+**
Region	88.9	44.1	52.9	74.2
Extra-region	11.1	27.1	22.9	6.5
No preference	-	28.8	24.2	19.3
Totals	100	100	100	100
	n=9	n=59	n=70	n=31

explanation is the fact that, first, a large number of members of the elite, especially from Jamaica, have been pursuing tertiary studies in extra-regional institutions. The data for both countries show that the ratio of percentage responses to preference for regional as against extra-regional education (Table 5.9) is significantly higher than that of percentage responses to family studying in regional as against extra-regional countries (Table 5.13). In the first case, the ratio is 4:1 while in the second it is 1:1.5 There seems to be a discrepancy between opinion and action.

Table 5.13: Family Actually Pursuing Tertiary Education
(Place and % Response)

Place	Jamaica n = 100	Saint Lucia n = 82
Region	43.0	29.3
Extra-region	27.0	17.1

West Indians have traditionally viewed education in the United Kingdom and the United States of America as superior to that offered in the region (Grant 1986). In fact, Grant has argued that this is one of the reasons why the University of West Indies in the past, and still presently, operates on the British university model.

This negative attitude seems to be reflected in data contained in Table 5.14 where preference for extra-regional education is based on its perceived superior quality and usefulness.

Table 5.14: Reasons for Preference for Extra-Regional
Education for Children
(% Response)

Reasons	Jamaica n=100	Saint Lucia n=82
Higher quality	22.0	20.7
More rounded education	19.0	17.1

Indeed, it is therefore not unreasonable to expect the elite, the group which has historically been impressed by foreign standards of culture, to prefer extra-regional over regional education (Phillips 1977), this attitude being most widespread among the economic elite (Tables 5.10, 5.11). This situation should not be surprising since, historically, the interests of this group have tended to converge with those of the bourgeoisie of the metropole, thereby resulting in attitudes which support the hegemony of the United States and the United Kingdom in the region. Such a relationship received a fillip during the 1950s and 1960s as a result of the "industrialization by invitation" strategy of economic development adopted by various Caribbean governments during the post World War II period. This approach to development received much criticism from economists such as Best and Thomas who argued that it only served to strengthen the relationship between the local bourgeoisie and the metropole at the expense of indigenous national development (Girvan and Jefferson 1976).

Since the 1940s the British Colonial Office, along with the political leadership of the region, saw education as a necessary prerequisite for independence and the development of the region along capitalist lines. This led to the formation of the University of the West Indies with its role becoming increasingly linked with providing qualified manpower for this process. According to Grant, from its inception, "the University was expected to provide the necessary political, administrative and technical leaders in a federated and ultimately independent West Indies" (Grant 1987:183).

However, the radicalism of the 1960s which "infected" the institution and caused the intellectuals to question the whole socio-economic order and propose radical solutions was to have a significantly negative impact on how the University of the West Indies was later to be perceived by members of the status quo (Grant 1987:187). Such negative perceptions are borne out by the responses of a number of respondents of the economic elite. Take, for example, the following two views:

> "the departments of social science and the economic division are usually staffed by communists who teach all sorts of ideological stupidity." (14)

> "the U.W.I. has to turn out, for want of a better word, a Caribbean man that we need, better than what has come out so far. For my own personal preference if I had to send my children [for tertiary education] I would send them to Canada, because I believe they would get a better overall grounding." (15)

It is probably these kinds of views which have led many members of the elite in the region to prefer extra-regional education in what they consider to be more prestigious and appropriate institutions.

Perhaps one case in which positive regionalist attitudes might have been reflected was in relation to respondents' views toward regional travel. But even then, some of the data contradict the claim.

For some time now, freedom of travel within the region has been recognized as an important ingredient for regional integration. For instance, this idea was strongly proposed under the Federation, although there was no effective strategy which allowed for the free movement of people from country to country (W.A. Lewis 1965). Bobb cites this as one of the shortcomings of the Federation, since there were no effective mechanisms in place which allowed for the continuous interaction of people from historically insular countries (Bobb 1966).

At present there is no provision within the CARICOM agreement for freedom of movement intra-regionally and member countries are still permitted to impose travel requirements without consultation with other member countries. One might, therefore, be tempted to infer a positive sign of regionalism when respondents from both countries, in the overwhelming majority, stated that they were in favour of the removal of travel restrictions between Caribbean countries (Table 5.15).

Table 5.15: Support for Removal of Travel Restrictions Within the Region
(% Response)

Response	Jamaica	Saint Lucia
No	8.0	3.7
Yes	83.0	85.4
Not sure	4.0	7.3
No response	5.0	3.6
Totals	100	100
	n=100	n=82

Those who were against the removal of restrictions gave one or two of the following reasons:

(1)   There is need to control the movement of people in order to lessen the chances of over-population of an individual country;

(2)   Countries are not ready for total freedom of travel;

(3)   The situation needs to be studied.

On the other hand, those who supported the removal of travel restrictions believed that this was one of the most important ways of showing regional integration. In fact, some respondents viewed full freedom of travel as a prerequisite for integration.

One cannot deny that the majority acceptance of respondents to uninhibited travel within the region is, to some extent, a reflection of their desire to strengthen regional unity. However, it is also true that a large number of the responses were not based on a desire to strengthen integration per se, but rather on previous negative travel experiences within the region. Many of these experiences resulted from strict travel regulations imposed by governments of the territories. For instance, in 1960 governments in territories such as Trinidad and Barbados imposed travel restrictions on intra-regional travel after the wave of intra-regional migration (Reubens 1962). The Windward and Leeward Islands were the countries mostly affected since they provided the bulk of the emigrants. Guyanese have found it difficult to travel within the region because a large number of them have been suspected of being engaged in illicit migration, mainly due to the political and economic crises in their country.

Since 1983 the Governments of Jamaica and Trinidad required Grenadians to have entry visas. They have subsequently eased such restrictions. It is therefore understandable why many respondents complained about the unsatisfactory treatment they received from customs and immigration officials. They were also displeased with the fact that American tourists required fewer travel documents than people of the region to enter most of the Caribbean countries. The following comments capture the feeling which a large number of respondents shared:

> "Freedom of movement is one of the biggest horrors ... as a result of my travels here in the Caribbean. It literally angers me, for example, when I am asked to let me see your ticket; how long are you going to stay; and a whole set of annoying questions." (16)

> "Going from Jamaica to Antigua we have to check through immigration, and going from Antigua to Montserrat we have to do likewise. This to me is very degrading, especially when foreigners from North America or Europe come to our shores without a passport." (17)

Overall, the data discussed above suggest that there is some amount of shared ideas about the region among the elite of the two countries. However, these ideas are very diffused, pointing to a weak regional identity. At the national and elite levels these ideas are more cohesive and structured for each country, thus indicating stronger national identities.

Explanation for Weak Regionalism

The foregoing discussion leads one to ask whether it is possible for people with such diverse perceptions of the region to arrive at a consensual explanation for the critical problems with which the regional integration movement is now faced. From the data it was found that the fact of varied perceptions has led to a number of different explanations.

It is the different and oftentimes conflicting ideological orientations that have led the regional political leadership to interpret and prescribe solutions for the problems of the region in different ways. For instance, the conflict between Manley and Williams over the nature of the federal structure during the Federation was partly a response to two different perceptions of the needs of the region (Bobb 1966). Manley's argument for a weak federal structure was a reflection of Jamaica's historical isolation from the region, in addition to Manley's view of the economic needs of the Jamaican community which could not be met through a federation. Trinidad's opposing position on the other hand reflected a closer sense of unity between the countries of the Eastern Caribbean and a perception of the need for greater interdependence within the region.

Further evidence of different interpretations of problems of the region was reflected in "radical" development paths adopted by Guyana, Jamaica and Grenada during the 1970s. All three countries adopted a non-capitalist path of development because their leadership did not perceive that full economic development could occur within the existing structures of dependent capitalism (Thomas 1987).

Many of the politicians who opposed these radical approaches were later to group themselves in the Caribbean Democratic Union (CDU) which was formed in 1986. The organization made up of prime ministers of Saint Christopher/Nevis, Dominica, Belize and Grenada emerged in opposition to radical political movements in the region with a view to consolidating free market capitalism (Best 1986). According to one supporter of the CDU:

> I am for capitalism and the Caribbean Democratic Union believes in that ideal ... I was once a wild eye radical on an American university campus and so I have seen life from both sides of the fence. I have come to understand what's good for the Caribbean and conservatism and capitalism would help us to grow and develop (*Caribbean Contact* 1985:4).

Evidence of the lack of any clear explanation for the problems of regionalism is reflected in the data. Although respondents were not asked directly to explain the reasons for the weakness of the regional movements, invariably, such responses occurred when they were asked to state what CARICOM was about, and whether it served a useful purpose.

Over 90 per cent of the respondents for each country saw the main role of CARICOM as facilitating economic integration and in this respect they saw it as being useful. However, there was a general feeling that CARICOM had failed to live up to expectations. Respondents gave a multiplicity of reasons for the failure of CARICOM. Overall, there were six different explanations (Table 5.16).

Table 5.16: Summary of Explanations for the Failure of CARICOM

Jamaica and Saint Lucia	
Explanations	**Percentage response**
1. Excessive nationalism	19.7
2. Lack of political will	25.2
3. Ideological differences	14.1
4. LDC/MDC differences	16.0
5. Improper development strategies	13.5
6. Need for more private sector involvement	11.3

These explanations, following the numerical order in Table 5.16, are captured in the following comments made by some of the respondents.

"My perception of CARICOM before I came here was that CARICOM was the Caribbean equivalent of EEC, which is basically a free trade area with political and social implications. Since I have been here, I have found that while that has been indeed the theoretical basis, the spirit in which it is interpreted is highly nationalistic." (18)

"CARICOM has not succeeded because the whole thing is so nebulous, fraught with suspicion, fraught with unwillingness of most political leaders to give up territorial control." (19)

"CARICOM has not worked because ideology has stood in the way." (20)

"CARICOM is a congregation of inefficient Caribbean producers whose Governments seemed to have conspired to keep their people in impoverishment on the basis that they are protecting local industry in order to develop capabilities of third country markets." (21)

"CARICOM has not really lived up to the kind of expectations of the founding members because CARICOM itself seems to have created occasions for fragmentating the integration process. It recognized, whether inadvertently or not, that within the grouping you have subgroups, you have MDC's and LDC's..." (22)

"CARICOM would be a good movement if there was less political interference and more of the private sector involvement." (23)

The most identifiable trend of the data is that reasons such as the lack of greater private sector involvement and improper development strategies were most common among the economic elite. On the other hand, the problem of LDC and MDC differences was a major concern of the Saint Lucian respondents.

The concerns of the economic elite seem to stem from the fact that trading tensions and conflicts have been a frequent feature of CARICOM relations. One might vividly recall the trade war between Jamaica, Trinidad and Guyana during the 1970s which led Eric Williams to set up what was then dubbed the "Tit for Tat Committee". Also, during the period, intra-regional trade plummetted as tensions between countries increased due partly to diverging political ideologies (Hippolyte-Manigat 1979). These tensions and conflicts continued throughout the eighties and became so critical that one writer has advised that "a political institutional mechanism, involving special areas of authority over individual CARICOM governments, is needed urgently if real progress is to be achieved" (Geiser 1977:32).

The concern of the Saint Lucian respondents with LDC/MDC differences reflects their unsatisfactory status within CARICOM. The polarization of intra-regional trade in favour of the MDCs and a declining economic and political relationship between the two groups of countries inevitably led to the formation of the OECS to protect their interest.

This dissatisfaction with the attitude of the MDCs is captured in a comment of a Saint Lucian respondent who states in reference to the need for political integration:

"...the bigger islands are not going into it unless they have something to benefit from it. And from past experiences the shark and sardines syndrome really works in these areas." (24)

However, these data demonstrate more than a lack of a shared explanation for the failure of regionalism. What they really show is that fragmentation and perpetual conflict characterize the regional movement, which above all, serves to reinforce the argument of the absence of an ideology of regionalism.

Towards Improved Regionalism: What is to be done?

If the data have so far confirmed that there is little coherence or consistency regarding perception and explanation, logically, it is hardly likely that there will be consensus with regard to action. In fact, one of the greatest areas of contention within the integration movement relates to the formulation of policies at the regional level (Hippolyte-Manigat 1979). The variation in priorities and different political ideologies, along with the changes brought on by the vicissitudes of the world's economy are some of the reasons why this process is made difficult. However, the major problem stems from the fact that there is no common regionalist ideological framework within which the policies are conceived and formulated. Eckstein has argued that political and economic relations within CARICOM have always been a source of conflict and have resulted from the different philosophical outlooks of the different countries, thus:

> operationally, the pursuit of different ideologies by CARICOM member countries has disturbed the philosophical and pragmatic bases for an economic union in a number of very fundamental ways ... the reality is that the imperatives involved in pursuit of different ideologies have tended to pull them farther apart (Samuel 1987:16).

This issue is clearly demonstrated by the fact that the countries of the movement have found it virtually impossible to present a common front in dealing with the external world. In addition, co-ordinated development planning and economic policies are also difficult to implement within the region because of different perceptions of development.

Insularity and parochialism have also played their part in frustrating regionalism. Eric Williams, during 1977, while stating his Government's opposition to bilateral aid, said: "if we are better placed then they, it is no particular fault of ours. The fact of the matter is that the Government of Trinidad and Tobago has a responsibility to the electorate, not to anybody's ideology" (Hippolyte-Manigat 1979:29).

In 1985 a trade dispute between Trinidad and Barbados resulted in the Barbadian soft drink manufacturers promoting their produce along nationalist lines. A number of advertisements were run on the media which implored Barbadians to purchase Barbadian made products since imported soft drinks did not contribute as much to their welfare. Such advertisements were aimed at undercutting Trinidad soft drink imports.

The Private Sector Organization of Jamaica has also promoted the manufacturers along similar lines. This is vividly demonstrated in one of their local slogans which states "buy Jamaican and put Jamaica first". So serious do nationalist concerns inhibit the development of regionalism, that Dr. R. Deosaran has argued: "This is indeed a tragic period for regionalism. The same condition which killed the Federation is now justifiably raising its deadly head once more: the spirit of nationalism" (Eckstein 1978:7).

The differences in philosophical outlook and also nationalistic attitudes have made it difficult for leaders to reach a consensus on the type of integration institutions required to strengthen regionalism. The recently proposed federation of the OECS has attracted much controversy among the political leadership of that part of the region. Although there seems to be general consensus on the principle of federation, the Standing Committee of Opposition Parties (SCOPE) does not agree with the proposed structure or with the way in which the leaders in office have set about to make the idea a reality *(The Vincentian* 27 November, 1987). SCOPE, unlike the more conservative ruling political parties is comprised of a number of left-leaning opposition political parties.

CARICOM leaders have reacted to Demas's recent call for political integration both positively and negatively. In 1986, Barrow and Hoyte expressed their support for the idea. However, Seaga was categorically opposed to the idea, while Charles said "I don't think it could be a reality now. I think we've missed the boat" *(Caribbean Contact* August 1986:9).

This lack of consensus among the political leaders also characterize the data on respondents' views on regional unity (Tables 5.17, 5.18). Interviewees were asked to respond to (i) type(s) of unity they would like to see; (ii) type of grouping most suitable for the region.

Table 5.17: Type of Unity Preferred
(% Response)

Type of unity preferred	Jamaica n=100	Saint Lucia n=82
Political	38.0	69.5
Economic	93.0	92.7
Cultural	66.0	72.0

In relation to the first question both Saint Lucian and Jamaican respondents showed the greatest preference for economic integration, although a considerably larger percentage of Saint Lucian respondents preferred political integration (Table 5.17). Responses to the second question indicated that while most Jamaican respondents saw functional co-operation as most suitable for the region, most Saint Lucians thought that more centralized types of unity in the form of political integration were best (Table 5.18).

Table 5.18: Type of Unity Considered Best for the Region
(% Response)

Type of Grouping	Jamaica n=100	Saint Lucia n=82
Functional co-operation	77.0	33.0
Federation	18.0	46.3
Unitary state	5.0	6.1

The greater preference among Saint Lucians for more centralized forms of integration points to the existence of comparatively stronger regionalist sentiment among them. To get an indication of this comparison, percentage responses to both questions were combined in a matrix resulting in a combination of two indicators — what respondents desired, and what they saw as best for the region. Using political integration as the highest expression of regionalism, the responses show higher overall scores for Saint Lucia (Table 5.19).

Table 5.19: Attitude to Political Integration for Region

Response	Per cent response	
	Jamaican n=100	St. Lucia n=82
Would prefer	38.0	70.7
Best for region	18.0	52.4

The stronger Saint Lucian sentiment may be explained by the fact that, historically and geographically, Saint Lucians have had close contacts with the countries of the Eastern Caribbean. The Jamaican responses on the other hand seem to reflect an opposite experience. Differences in opinion over what type of integration is best for the region also occurred across elite groups. This was more the situation with the Saint Lucian data as the

Jamaican data showed a much more even distribution of responses (Tables 5.20, 5.21). The most noticeable feature of the Saint Lucian responses is that the economic elite gave the highest percentage responses in favour of federation.

Table 5.20: Type of Unity Thought Best for Region

Jamaica			
Type of unity	Cultural	Economic	Political
Functional co-operation	71.9	78.9	80.0
Federation	18.7	18.4	20.0
Unitary State	3.1	-	-
Non-response	6.2	2.6	-
Totals	100	100	100
	n=33	n=38	n=30

Table 5.21: Type of unity thought best for region

Saint Lucia			
Type of unity	Cultural	Economic	Political
Functional co-operation	35.5	29.1	34.6
Federation	45.2	54.2	42.3
Unitary State	6.4	-	-
Non-response	12.9	12.5	15.4
Totals	100	100	100
	n=31	n=24	n=26

The uniformity among Jamaican elite responses indicates a majority negative attitude toward political integration across all elite groups. Witness, for example, some of the commonly shared comments from three respondents:

"What is more feasible is what exists right now because feasibility is a direct function of political willingness." (25).

"Political integration will not happen between Jamaica, Barbados, Trinidad and Guyana. Anybody who thinks that this will happen is living in a dream world." (26)

"There has been a mishap with federation which as you know suffered a setback in 1962...I think nerves are too raw to proceed along the same lines, emphasis has to be the other way, functional co-operation." (27)

The majority positive attitude toward political integration among the Saint Lucian economic elite may be explained in two ways. First, there seemed to be a greater preference for a federation of the OECS countries rather than of the entire Caribbean community. This point is captured in the views of one respondent who states:

"I think that a federation leads to strength, you have more clout, you speak as one body rather than individually ... I think this is moreso for the OECS than the rest of the West Indies. I definitely support the proposed OECS federation." (28)

Secondly, a federation of the OECS has recently received substantial support from some of the region's leading intellectuals such as William Demas (1987). In addition, some governments of the OECS have endorsed the federal idea. According to much of the current thinking in that part of the region, political integration is the most effective way of achieving development goals. The fact that the Saint Lucia Chamber of Commerce has given official support to the idea of OECS federation would suggest that the commercial sector expects to benefit from such a process. It would appear, therefore, that many business persons share Demas's view that a political union could allow for a single unified common market for goods and services, capital and manpower. Additionally, freedom of movement of capital carries with it the right of a person or company in any OECS territory to establish his business in other OECS states (Demas 1987). These two explanations become more plausible if one considers that this elite group gave the lowest positive overall percentage response to the question on the existence of a Caribbean identity but yet the highest percentage response to preference for political and economic integration. One might infer that the response to the question on type of unity preferred may have been based, fundamentally, on pragmatic economic considerations instead of a genuine commitment to regionalism. This comment from a respondent captures the crux of the economic argument:

"Many islands in the Caribbean have a population of approximately one hundred thousand. I cannot see how a nation state can be financially viable if it is that small." (29)

Another feature of the variation in the data relates to the skewed distribution of the responses according to age group. In both the Saint Lucian and Jamaican samples, respondents in the 36-45 age group gave the largest percentage of favourable responses to federation (Fig. 5.1). Those under 36 years seemed least in favour of political integration.

Using percentage responses to functional co-operation, federation and unitary state as indicators of integration sentiment, an indication of the relationship of such sentiments between the age groups for both countries combined is obtained (Fig. 5.2).

The apparent comparatively greater preference for stronger forms of integration among the 36-45 age group is probably a result of the influence of the Federation era. The influence of federalist sentiments may be seen as important since, as Inglehart (1967:329) argues: "an individual's sense of national identity seems to have a tendency to be formed early and to persist through later life."

Further, he has shown that changes in conditions of socialization according to age group have led to differences in the degree of support for European integration. Those who received basic socialization during the period of high European nationalism, just before the Second World War, were generally against supranationalism. On the other hand, those who received their basic socialization after the Second World War showed highly favourable attitudes toward supranationalism. Additionally, Jean Piaget has found that Swiss children had generally formed a sense of national identity by the age of twelve (Piaget and Weil 1951).

Using the arguments of Piaget and Inglehart, one may conclude that respondents in the 36-45 age group would have been more likely to be socialized within a supranational environment than the members of the other age groups and therefore would have reflected such sentiment in their responses. Respondents in this age group would have been between the ages of 6 and 16, perhaps the most critical part of the socialization stage when the Federation officially began.

The age group differences combined with those among elite groups and countries, by implication, illustrate that there is a lack of consensus within the region on what is to be done to improve the integration movement. Indeed, it must be made clear that for there to be consensus on the type of action needed to improve the movement, there must first be agreement on the nature of the movement. The data show that this is a highly contentious issue.

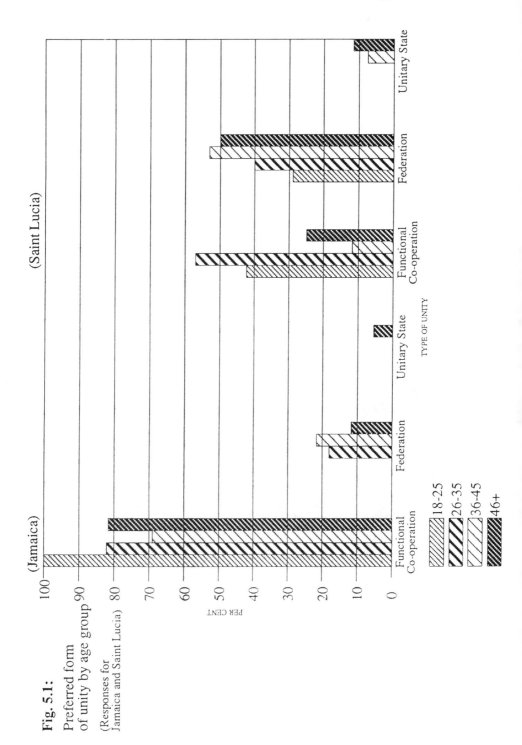

Fig. 5.1:

Preferred form
of unity by age group

(Responses for
Jamaica and Saint Lucia)

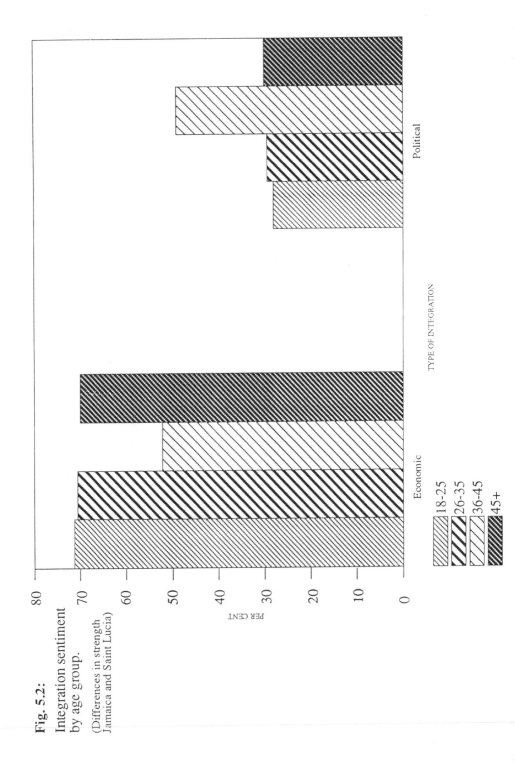

Fig. 5.2:

Integration sentiment
by age group.

(Differences in strength
Jamaica and Saint Lucia)

Conclusions

The discussion has so far attempted to demonstrate that among the elite of Saint Lucia and Jamaica there is no organized body of perceptions, explanations and actions about regionalism that can be called an ideology. Instead, what exists are a number of perceptions, explanations and prescriptions which vary, in many cases significantly, both between and within the two countries.

In many cases, these attitudes reflect the existence of regionalist sentiment, the strength of which varies according to country and elite group. The existence of these ideas and mental images about the region and regional integration can be referred to as ideation. The discussion has also shown that this ideation process is at a higher level in Saint Lucia as Saint Lucian respondents show a stronger regionalist orientation and seem to demonstrate a greater degree of commitment to regionalism. Overall, the economic elite demonstrate the weakest regional sentiment, and the least positive attitudes toward regionalism.

The ability of the region to develop an ideology of regionalism is frustrated by two major factors, namely, the historical development of the region where the territories, perhaps with the exception of those of the Windward and Leeward Islands, developed as fragmented and insular units under the hegemonic control of Britain and, in more recent times following the Second World War, the development of the hegemonic relationship between the region and the United States of America which has caused the region to come under American economic and cultural domination.

The first issue has been already dealt with at length in chapter 2. In reiterating the argument, it is important to point out that it was this insular development of the individual territories in the region, integrated into the economy of the mother country, which militated against political unity.

The data already presented do in fact confirm that, to a large extent, this insularity still exists. In reference to the second point, it is difficult to overstate the role and tremendous influence of the United States of America militarily, economically and culturally in the region (V.A. Lewis 1984).

Although comparatively recent, the United States of America's involvement in the region has been significant. Gordon Lewis, for example, argues that American interests in the region date back to the very foundation of the Republic. This interest was, primarily, in the area of trade and became even more important with the building of the Panama Canal which became the key to the commercial expansion of the Pacific (G. Lewis 1968).

According to Vaughan Lewis, a fundamental concern of the United States of America for the area "lies in its strategic significance for the maintenance of her own natural security" (1984:7). In addition, the United States of America is "concerned to ensure the uninterrupted conduct of the trade in the Caribbean mineral resources, in particular bauxite (ibid.). It is for such reasons, he continues, that, "assertions of Sovereign rights by Caribbean states are accepted as legitimate, or are deemed momentarily subordinate to the protection of the U.S. interests" (ibid.:8).

Arising out of this situation is the development of a relationship between the economic elite of the region and the United States of America where this group perceives its interests as being inextricably intertwined with American interests in the region. Thomas is referring to such a relationship when he states that a major limitation of CARICOM is that it represents, ".... the partnership (dependency) of national capital with imperialist capital" (Thomas 1979:285). It is this relationship which in large part accounts for the weak regionalist sentiment among the economic elite.

One of the important ways in which United States hegemony manifests itself is at the level of ideology where there is a fundamental impact on the attitudes of people. The cultural impact of the American society is so tremendous that a study commissioned by the Caribbean Publishing and Broadcasting Association (CPBA) advised that it was vital that action be taken to broaden the choice available to Caribbean television audiences.

One reason for this piece of advice resulted from the fact that American programming was seen as having a negative impact on the development of a West Indian culture and identity (*The Weekend Voice* 13 February 1988). The omnipresence of American lifestyle in the region is in large part due to what Hamelink calls transnational cultural synchronization. The principal agents of this process are transnational corporations, largely based in the United States of America, which are involved in global investment through international communications firms (Hamelink 1983). The threat to cultural autonomy and national and regional identity by cultural synchronization was highlighted in 1973 during a conference in Algiers of non-aligned countries: "...it is an established fact that the activity of imperialism is not limited to economic and political domains, but that it encompasses social and cultural areas as well, imposing thereby a foreign ideological domination on the peoples of the developing world" (Hamelink 1983:26).

A corollary of this process of hegemony is that the dominated people may develop strong loyalties and attachments to the dominating country, which result in weaker national or regional sentiments. Indeed, there seems to be support for this argument in the data.

For example, respondents were asked to name three countries to which they felt most attached. Initially, respondents were asked to rank the countries. However, because they had difficulty in doing so, they were asked simply to name the countries. Interestingly, the five countries with the highest number of responses were similar for both Jamaica and Saint Lucia. The lower percentages for Saint Lucia are due to a comparatively higher level of non-response to this question. Using percentage response as a measure of the level of attachment, an "attachment scale" is constructed for both countries (Table 5.22).

Table 5.22: Levels of Attachment to Foreign Countries

Scale ranking	Jamaica		Saint Lucia	
	Country	%	Country	%
1	U.S.A.	44	U.K.	26.8
2	U.K.	23	Barbados	20.7
3	Trinidad	21	U.S.A.	17.1
4	Canada	14	Canada	15.9
5	Barbados	13	Trinidad	14.6

The order of these countries shows that except for Barbados, extra-regional countries ranked the highest. Of more fundamental concern is the fact that only two Caribbean countries were among the group.

In both countries the cultural and economic elite felt most attached to extra-regional countries (Figs. 5.3, 5.4). Only in the case of the political elite of Saint Lucia was there strongest attachment to a Caribbean country.

Using responses in Fig. 5.5 as a guide to a comparison of attachment levels between elite groups, the evidence shows that, overall, the economic elite felt most attached to extra-regional countries while the political elite felt most attached to countries within the region.

When asked for the ways in which they felt attached to these countries, respondents from both countries cited family ties and the culture of the country.

These findings are not totally consistent with the argument advanced by Wiltshire-Brodber that within the region there exists a core set of

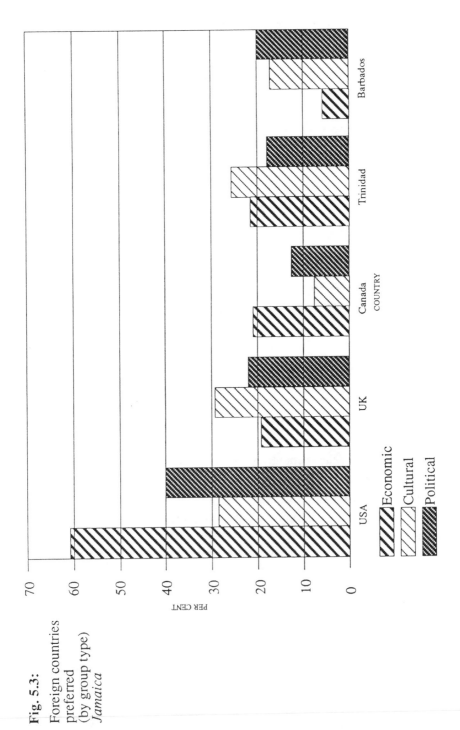

Fig. 5.3:
Foreign countries
preferred
(by group type)
Jamaica

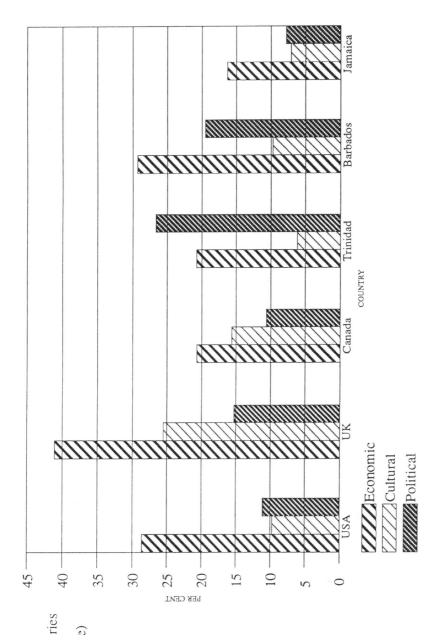

Fig. 5.4:

Foreign countries
preferred
(by group type)
Saint Lucia

Fig. 5.5: Attachment levels among elite groups

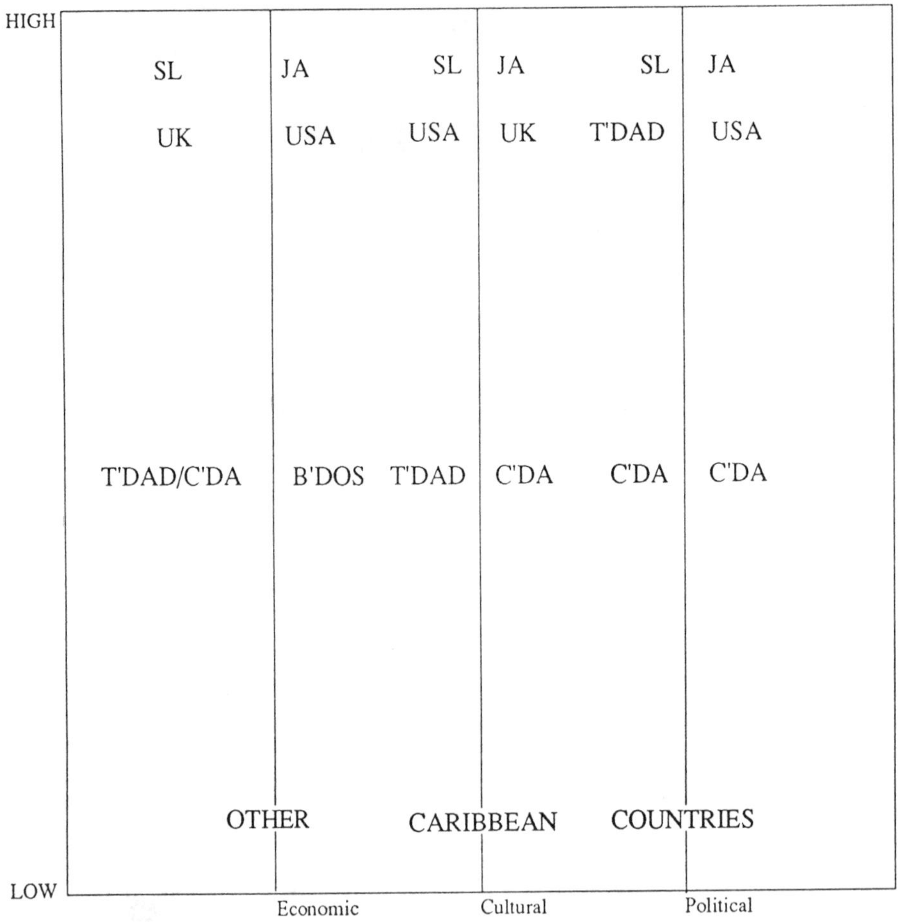

SL = Saint Lucia
JA = Jamaica

Fig. 5.6: Caribbean integration - Relative relationships
with Saint Lucia and Jamaica

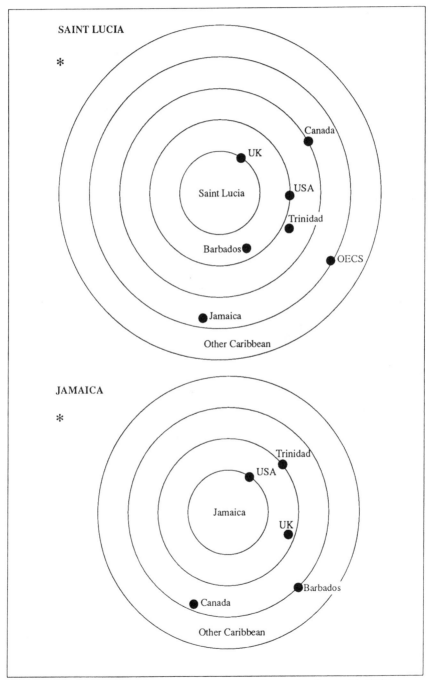

* Note that degree of integration decreases as you move away from centre of concentric circles.

countries which are well integrated outside of the formal structures of the integration movement, with the United States of America and the United Kingdom on the periphery (Wiltshire-Brodber 1984). The relationship between these countries is shown by a set of concentric circles (Appendix VI). This core set of countries consists of Trinidad at the centre with Barbados and the OECS countries. These countries, she argues, are linked by loyalties developed through family ties and intra-regional migration.

Admittedly, Wiltshire-Brodber's paper deals with a mass study. However, it is difficult to imagine, given the history of the region, the United Kingdom and the United States of America as being on the periphery. In addition, there has been a significant amount of migration from the Caribbean to extra-regional countries. In fact, during the period of the greatest wave of intra-regional migration, 1957-1960, some countries experienced higher net outflows to the United Kingdom and the United States of America than to countries of the region (Reubens 1962). This is certainly true for Saint Lucia, Saint Christopher/Nevis and Jamaica (Appendixes VII, VIII). Finally, the above data show that for respondents of both countries, the attachment to extra-regional countries is overwhelming relative to countries of the region. This suggests that both the United States of America and the United Kingdom are very much "part of" the region. It is true that writers have tended to define the region as comprising countries within the Caribbean Basin itself, and it is quite possible that people of the region might see the region is such a way. However, no empirical evidence exists to support such a claim.

Based on the view that there exists a strong correlation between elite and mass attitudes (see, for example, Boggs 1976), Figure 5.6 gives an alternative interpretation of the integration relations of the region. The figure shows that the United States of America and the United Kingdom are strongly integrated into the region. A clear implication of this situation is that for the region to develop an ideology of regionalism, the hegemony of these two countries will have to be countered.

CHAPTER 6

Summary and Conclusions

The evidence arising out of this study supports the main hypothesis that the Caribbean regional integration movement is weak and unstable because it is not based upon nor is it guided by an ideology of regionalism. The major reason for this is that, historically, the pursuit of regional integration as a process has been seen simply as a means to an end but never as an end in itself. As has been shown in chapter 3, the motive behind early forms of regional integration had been, initially, to achieve administrative efficiency and, later, economic viability so as to facilitate constitutional independence. Hence, when some countries which were members of the Federation discovered that it was possible to achieve economic viability and consequently independence without a political union, regionalism was eschewed for insular national development. The discussion in chapter 4 indicates that later attempts at regional integration were restricted to pragmatic forms of economic and functional co-operation through CARIFTA and, later, CARICOM. The rationale for such pragmatism was that countries would be able to maintain individual autonomy over national development as the convergence of political and economic interests of the different territories would ultimately lead to co-operation and a harmonious regional relationship to the benefit of all parties. The weight of the evidence has, however, contradicted such a view, pointing instead to the ever-present conflict in all areas of regional co-operation and the perpetual emasculation of the principles and spirit of the CARICOM Treaty.

Perhaps, the greatest support for the hypothesis can be found in chapter 5 where a discussion of elite attitudes towards integration in Saint Lucia and Jamaica indicates that there is no ideology of regionalism but simply the existence of regionalist ideation. Admittedly, one has to be cautious in generalizing the findings to the entire region and among all social groups, since the survey was restricted to only one social group within two countries. Notwithstanding this caveat, when the survey findings are combined with the arguments advanced in chapters 3 and 4, one can hardly deny the extremely high possibility of there being similar results within most, if not all, of the other territories. Additionally, in view of the fact of elite domination of social, political and economic institutions resulting in their hegemony over the masses, it seems highly improbable that mass attitudes will be significantly different from those found in the survey.

The case for regional integration has been made by a number of writers most of whom have emphasized either political or/and economic variables. A review of the literature has however revealed that too little attention has been paid to the role of ideology in the integration process. Although there has been some discussion of the role of ideology in regional integration, this has been confined mainly to a discussion of partisan political ideology and not addressed specifically to regionalism as an autonomous process. If Caribbean social theory is to have any fundamental impact on improving and deepening the regional integration process then, based on the above discussion, one cannot gainsay the need for greater research and theorising on the role of ideology in promoting regional integration.

Arising out of the study there are a number of specific measures which could be pursued to further the development of an ideology of regionalism. Such measures are characterized by their ability to promote a strong regional identity, cohesion and interdependence. They would allow for sustained interaction among the people of the region, socially and culturally, at all levels of society. One such area to which regional policy makers and researchers can turn their immediate attention is to that of mass communications. One of the most effective avenues for sharing and developing ideas is through the media. As the data in chapter 5 show, the media have been one of the greatest sources of cultural diffusion within the region. The dominance of the United States in this area has ultimately contributed to the strengthening of their hegemony in the region. It is therefore highly likely that the development of the region's telecommunications system to promote greater interaction between Caribbean people could go a long way in strengthening regional consciousness, a necessary step towards the advancement of an ideology of regionalism.

Efforts have been made in the area through the Caribbean Broadcasting Union (CBU), the Caribbean News Agency (CANA) and the establishment of the Caribbean Institute of Mass Communications (CARIMAC) at the Mona Campus of the UWI. Both the CBU and CANA have done an excellent job in bringing the region closer together by informing the territories about each other. The CBU's role at the 1996 Atlanta Olympics, where it brought a Caribbean perspective to the Games, no doubt gave the people of the region a sense of pride and self-confidence. While such steps are an important start in the right direction, they will not suffice since these institutions only cover a small section of the region's population. Perhaps greater consideration should be given to the creation of a Caribbean radio station which broadcasts to the entire anglophone Caribbean region on a regular basis. Its programmes would heighten the awareness of people in each territory about the region and allow for greater discussion and development of ideas. Consideration could also be given to the setting up of a Caribbean film making organization committed to tapping the endless talent of Caribbean writers, producers, actors and artistes. The Edna Manley College of the Performing and Visual Arts in Jamaica has trained some of the leading artistes in the region, some of whom have been forced to migrate to metropolitan countries because of the lack of opportunities in the performing arts. Attempts by entrepreneurs and artistes to produce films at the national level have been costly. Nevertheless, with an expanding market and a larger resource endowment, economies of scale would result making the venture more viable. The establishment of a film making company producing Caribbean films, apart from offering economic opportunities, would be a positive response to the dominance of American programming in the region and a further step towards the development of an ideology of regionalism.

Music is also a potential source of integration. Apart from cricket, Caribbean music is probably the single most important source of cultural interaction among the peoples of the region. Calypso and reggae are both important features of the region's unique identity in the eyes of extra-regional countries. A booming entertainment industry across the region has resulted in the creative integration of music and ideas from Jamaica to Guyana. New forms of music are emerging, and along with it new ways of marketing these products. Calypsonians and industry investors are taking a regional and international approach to the production and dissemination of the music. Artistes in the region are showing how cultural activity can contribute to greater economic integration and development. Interestingly, from the survey, many respondents revealed that music was an important source of attachment to other Caribbean counties. For example, some St. Lucian respondents' only form of identification with Jamaica was through reggae music. It is therefore clear that the creation of a vibrant regional music industry which encourages and promotes regional music among the people can augur well for regional integration.

The above are only a few suggestions for increasing intra-regional interaction mainly at the social and cultural levels, although it is clear that there are many economic benefits to be derived from them. However, the adoption of such measures presupposes the existence of the political will to implement them, and greater coordination and cohesion of government policy at the regional level. Of course, the implementation of some of these measures by non-governmental bodies could also lead to the development of a stronger regionalist orientation among the political leadership of the region.

The scope for greater and sustained regional interaction is almost limitless, a major reason for this being that the implementation of any one regionalist policy should have a trickle-down effect on other policies. The sum total of these measures with a distinct regional bias would, at the very least, encourage people of the individual territories, both at the mass and elite level, to give greater consideration to the impact of national policy formulation on the other countries of the region. Ideally, it should lead to the realization of an attitude and resultant policies by all the territories which accept that the development of each individual country is inextricably intertwined with regional development as a whole.

Appendixes

APPENDIX 1: INTRA-AREA TRADE AND THE GROSS DOMESTIC PRODUCT, 1967-72

	Imports from CARIFTA as % of GDP			Exports to CARIFTA as % of GDP		
	1967	1970	1972	1967	1970	1972
Barbados	7.0	9.9	12.5	2.9	4.1	6.4
Guyana	6.9	8.1	9.9	5.9	5.7	8.4
Jamaica	0.5	0.8	2.3	0.7	1.1	1.5
Trinidad	1.2	1.6	2.0	3.3	5.0	5.7
ECCM*	13.3	19.2	19.4	2.3	2.3	3.1
CARIFTA*	2.5	3.4	4.4	2.3	3.1	3.9

*Excludes Belize

Source: A. Payne, The Politics of the Caribbean Community 1961-79, (Manchester, U.K.: Manchester University Press, 1980).

APPENDIX II: VALUE OF INTRA-REGIONAL IMPORTS (US$ MILLION) AND AS PERCENTAGE OF TOTAL IMPORTS OF CARICOM COUNTRIES

	1973	%	1974	%	1975	%	1976	%
Barbados	21.8	13.0	35.2	17.3	3.4	17.7	41.0	17.3
Guyana	38.7	22.1	0.3	26.4	73.6	21.3	48.5	13.3
Jamaica	35.3	5.2	71.5	7.6	94.4	8.4	63.8	6.6
Trinidad	20.5	2.6	30.1	1.6	42.1	2.8	53.7	2.7
MDCs	116.3	6.4	204.1	6.3	245.5	7.76	207.0	5.8
LDCs	29.5	13.9	43.2	16.2	36.2	13.2	36.2	n.a
Total								
CARICOM	145.8	7.2	247.3	7.1	281.7	8.2	243.2	n.a.

Source: M. Hippolyte-Manigat, "Crises in CARICOM or the CARICOM Crisis". Paper presented at the International Conference on the Caribbean, Mexico City, 20-25 August 1979.

APPENDIX III: VALUE OF INTRA-REGIONAL EXPORTS (US$ MILLION) AND AS PERCENTAGE OF TOTAL EXPORTS OF CARICOM COUNTRIES

	1973	%	1974	%	1975	%	1976
Barbados	14.4	27.2	18.4	21.6	19.6	18.4	22.8
Guyana	20.1	14.9	29.7	11.2	44.0	12.5	30.0
Jamaica	24.5	6.2	32.3	4.4	33.0	4.2	43.2
Trinidad	76.9	10.0	140.8	6.9	159.7	8.9	161.5
MDCs	135.9	10.6	221.2	7.1	256.3	8.4	257.5
LDCs	9.1	8.9	15.0	11.2	n.a.	-	n.a.
Total							
CARICOM	145.0	10.5	236.2	7.2	-	-	-

Source: M. Hippolyte-Manigat, ibid.

APPENDIX IV: TRADE POLARISATION BETWEEN
MDCs AND LDCs

IMPORTS

YEAR	MDCs	LDCs
1973	79.6	20.5
1974	82.6	17.4
1975	87.1	12.9
1976	85.1	14.9

EXPORTS

YEAR	MDCs	LDCs
1973	93.7	6.3
1974	95.3	4.7
1975	-	-
1976	-	-

Source: Hippolyte-Manigat, ibid.

APPENDIX V: TRADE AMONG THE MDCs

Imports %

Year	Barbados		Guyana		Jamaica		Trinidad	
1973	18.7	(14.9)	33.3	(26.5)	30.4	(24.2)	17.6	(14.1)
1974	17.2	(14.2)	33.0	(27.2)	35.0	(28.9)	14.7	(12.2)
1975	14.4	(12.6)	30.0	(26.1)	38.5	(33.5)	17.1	(14.9)
1976	19.8	(18.9)	23.4	(19.9)	30.8	(26.2)	25.9	(22.1)

( ) % of total intra-regional imports

Exports %

Year	Barbados		Guyana		Jamaica		Trinidad	
1973	10.6	(9.9)	14.8	(13.9)	18.0	(16.9)	56.7	(53.0)
1974	8.3	(7.9)	13.4	(12.8)	14.6	(13.9)	63.7	(60.7)
1975	7.6	-	17.2	-	12.9	-	62.3	-
1976	8.9	-	11.7	-	16.8	-	62.7	-

( ) % of total intra-regional exports

Source: M. Hippolyte-Manigat, ibid.

APPENDIX VI   CARIBBEAN INTEGRATION
- A NEW PERSPECTIVE

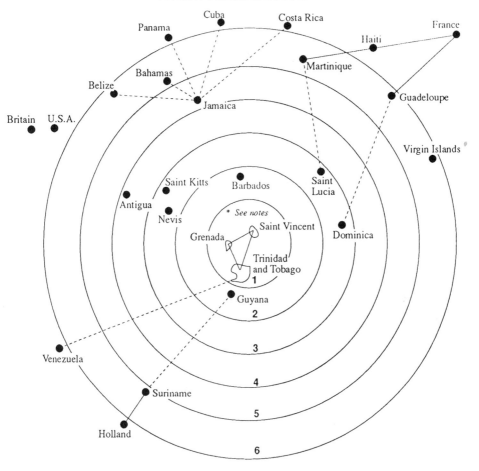

STRONGLY INTEGRATED INNER CORE - VERY STRONG
POLITICAL ECONOMIC AND SOCIAL LINKAGES

1. Multiple Loyalties
2. Free Movement of Labour and Capital
3. Strong Trade Ties
4. Shared Services
5. High Level of Political Participation
6. Common Language, Culture and History

Note (a) Links decreased as one moves towards the outer edge of concentric circles.
It is possible to identify several different codes within the Eastern
Caribbean with Trinidad and Tobago, Grenada and Saint Vincent merely
representative of the relationships existing among them.

Note (b) Reprinted, with permission, from R. Wiltshire-Brodber, "What role do Caribbean people play in promoting
regional integration?" In *Ten Years of CARICOM*   (Washington, D.C., 1984), 183-200

APPENDIX VII: NET POPULATION MOVEMENTS IN EACH TERRITORY IN 1959 (OVERALL, INTRA-FEDERATION AND TO THE UNITED KINGDOM)

Territory	A	B	C	D
Saint Vincent	80,005	-1,538	-1,073	-353
Grenada	88,617	-2,175	n.a.	n.a.
Barbados	232,085	-1,039	2,488	n.a.
Saint Lucia	86,184	-1,145	-97	-1,012
Saint Christopher Nevis	56,644	-1,061	131	-866
Trinidad	825,700	4,845	6,284	-1,497
Jamaica	1,606,000	-16,300	-56	-10,478

Column A: Population on census day 7 April 1960.
Column B: The net overall movement to each island.
Column C: The net intra-Federation movement for each island.
Column D: The net migration to the United Kingdom for each island.

Source: E.P. Reubens, *Migration and development in the West Indies* (Mona, Jamaica: ISER, 1962).

APPENDIX VIII: NET POPULATION MOVEMENTS IN EACH TERRITORY JANUARY-JUNE 1960:
(OVERALL, INTRA-FEDERATION AND TO THE UNITED KINGDOM)

Territory	A	B	C	D
Saint Vincent	80,005	-221	-235	-571
Grenada	88,617	-1,153	n.a.	-832
Barbados	232,085	-693	1,512	n.a.
Saint Lucia	86,194	-1,002	-401	-908
Saint Christopher Nevis	56,644	-1,650	-589	n.a.
Trinidad	825,700	227	825	1,260
Jamaica	1,606,000	-10,882	-243	-11,629

Column A: Population on census day 7 April 1960.
Column B: The net overall movement to each island.
Column C: The net intra-Federation movement for each island.
Column D: The net migration to the United Kingdom for each island.

Source: E.P. Reubens, *Migration and development in the West Indies* (Mona, Jamaica:ISER, 1962)

APPENDIX IX: RESPONDENT KEY

(01)   Radio broadcaster (Jamaica).

(02)   Executive director of a private commercial interest group (Jamaica).

(03)   Church administrator (Jamaica).

(04)   Senior civil servant (Saint Lucia).

(05)   Director of culture (Saint Lucia).

(06)   Political activist and member of opposition party (Saint Lucia).

(07)   Managing director of a commercial enterprise (Jamaica).

(08)   Teacher and administrator of performing arts school (Jamaica).

(09)   Manager and programme director of a radio station (Jamaica).

(10)   Director of a training institution for mass communications.

(11)   Managing director of a commercial enterprise (Saint Lucia).

(12)   Managing director of a commercial enterprise (Saint Lucia).

(13)   Manager of a commercial enterprise (Saint Lucia).

(14)   Same as (02).

(15)   Chairman of board of directors of a commercial enterprise (Saint Lucia).

(16)   Director of government statutory corporation (Saint Lucia).

(17)   Managing director of a commercial enterprise (Jamaica).

(18)   Managing director of a commercial enterprise (Saint Lucia).

(19)   University lecturer (Jamaica).

(20)   Minister of government (Saint Lucia).

(21)   Same as (02).

(22)   Manager of a commercial enterprise (Jamaica).

(23)   Manager of a commercial enterprise (Jamaica).

(24)   Political activist and member of opposition party (Saint Lucia).

(25)   Same as (12).

(26)   Manager of a commercial enterprise (Saint Lucia).

(27)   Political activist and member of opposition party (Jamaica).

(28)   Managing director of a commercial enterprise (Saint Lucia).

(29)   Managing director of a commercial enterprise (Saint Lucia).

Bibliography

Anderson, A. 1988. "Crisis Diplomacy in the Commonwealth Caribbean: Anguilla (1967); Grenada (1983); Haiti (1983)." Paper presented at the First Conference of Caribbean Graduate Students, 15-16 April, University of the West Indies, Mona.

Axline, A. 1979. *Caribbean Integration: The Politics of Regionalism*, New York: Nicholls Publishing Co.

Barbados Advocate News. 1977. 26 February, Bridgetown, Barbados.

Beckford, G., and M. Witter. 1985. *Small Garden, Bitter Weed*, Morant Bay, Jamaica: Maroon Publishing House.

Bennett, K. 1984. "Balance of Payments Policies and Caribbean Integration." Paper prepared for the Sixteenth Annual Conference of the Regional Programme of Monetary Studies, October, Kingston, Jamaica.

Bernal, R., M. Budhai, and P. Gordon. 1984. *Jamaica and the Economic Crisis in CARICOM*, Department of Economics, University of the West Indies, Mona, mimeo.

Best, T. 1986. "Caribbean Searching for Models", *Caribbean Contact* (November).

Bobb, L. 1966. "The Federal Principle in the British West Indies: An Appraisal of Its Use", *Social and Economic Studies* 16 (3).

Boggs, C. 1976. *Gramsci's Marxism*, New York: Plato Press.

Bottomore, T. 1966. *Elites and Society*, Harmondsworth: Penguin Books.

Brathwaite, L. 1974. *Social Stratification in Trinidad*, Mona, Jamaica: ISER.

Brown, A., and R. Sanatan. 1987. *Talking to Whom?* Mona, Jamaica: University of the West Indies, CARIMAC.

Burnham, F. 1970. "We Must Integrate or Perish" in *A Destiny to Mould: Selected Discourses by the Prime Minister of Guyana*, London.

The Caribbean Community in the 1980s. 1981. Georgetown, Guyana: CARICOM Secretariat.

Caribbean Contact. (March) 1984.

—————. (March) 1985.

—————. (July) 1987.

Clarke, C. 1984. "Caribbean Consciousness" in *Perspectives on Caribbean Regional Identity*, ed. E. Thomas-Hope. Liverpool: University of Liverpool, Centre for Latin American Studies.

Coard, B. 1978. "The Meaning of Political Independence in the Commonwealth Caribbean", in *Independence for Grenada: Myth or Reality?* Proceedings of Conference on the Implications of Independence for Grenada, edited by the Conference Committee, St. Augustine, Trinidad: Institute of International Relations, 11-12 January 1974.

Daily Gleaner. 1977. 10 May, Kingston, Jamaica.

DeCastro, S. 1967. *Problems of the Caribbean Air Transport Industry*, Mona, Jamaica: ISER.

Demas, W. 1965. *The Economics of Development in Small Countries with Special Reference to the Caribbean*, Montreal: McGill University Press.

—————. 1972. *From CARIFTA to the Caribbean Community*, Georgetown, Guyana: Commonwealth Regional Secretariat.

—————. 1974. *West Indian Nationhood and Caribbean Integration*, Bridgetown, Barbados: CCC Publishing House.

—————. 1976. *Essays on Caribbean Integration and Development*, Mona, Jamaica: ISER.

—————. 1987. *Seize the Time: Towards OECS Political Union,* based on an address at the inauguration of the National Advisory Committee of St. Vincent and the Grenadines on Political Unity in the Grenadines, 26 August, Saint Michael, Barbados.

Deosaran, R. 1984. "Nationalism vs. CARICOM", *Caribbean Contact* (April).

Deutsch, K. 1972. "Attaining and Maintaining Integration" in *European Integration,* edited by M. Hodges. Harmondsworth: Penguin Books.

Duncan, N. 1987. "The Georgetown Declaration", *CARICOM Perspective* January-March.

Eagleton, T. 1983. *Marxism and Literary Criticism*, London: Methuen.

Eckstein, J. 1978. "CARICOM: An Evaluation of its Prospects for Survival", *Caribbean Monthly Bulletin* (4-5) April-May, Supplement.

Etzioni, A. 1965. *Political Unification*, New York: Holt, Rinehart and Winston.

Europe in Figures. 1988. Eurostat, Luxembourg: Office of the Official Publications of the European Communities.

Farrell, T. 1983. "CARICOM at the Crossroads", *Caribbean Contact* (June).

Geiser, H. 1977. *A Short Summary of the CARICOM Treaty* , Mona, Jamaica: University of the West Indies.

Girvan, N., and O. Jefferson. 1976. *Essays on Caribbean Integration and Development*, Mona, Jamaica: ISER.

Gittens, T. 1983. "The Politics of Commonwealth Caribbean Regional Integration: Review Article", *CARICOM Bulletin* (3), Georgetown, Guyana: CARICOM Secretariat.

Grandison, G. 1988. "No to Backdoor Federation", *Daily Gleaner* (2 July).

Grant, R. 1987. "The Politics of Higher Education within a Regional Context: The Caribbean Community and Common Market (CARICOM)", *Journal of Commonwealth and Comparative Politics* 25(2): 180-95.

Gyorgy, A., and G. Blackwood. 1976. *Ideologies in World Affairs*, London: Blaisdell Publishing Co.

Haas, E. 1972. "International Integration", in *European Integration*, edited by M. Hodges. Harmondsworth: Penguin Books.

Hall, K., and B. Blake. 1976. "Major Developments in CARICOM". *1975 Caribbean Yearbook of International Relations*, Leyden: A.W. Sijthhoff; Saint Augustine, Trinidad: University of the West Indies, Institute of International Relations.

Hamelink, C.J. 1983. *Cultural Autonomy in Global Communications*, New York and London: Longmans.

Hansen, R. 1972. "Regional Integration: Reflections on a Decade of Theoretical Efforts" in *European Integration*, edited by M. Hodges. Harmondsworth: Penguin Books.

Hippolyte-Manigat, M. 1979. "Crises in CARICOM or the CARICOM Crisis?" Paper presented at the International Conference on the Caribbean, 20-25 August, Mexico City.

Hodges, M. ed. 1972. *European Integration*, Harmondsworth: Penguin Books.

Hoffman, S. 1966. "Obstinate or Obsolete? The Fate of the Nation State and the Case of Western Europe", *Daedalus* 95: 862-915.

Inglehart, R. 1967. "An End to European Integration", *American Political Science Review* 61 (1).

Kinshasa, K. 1984. "Interview with Maurice Bishop", *The Black Scholar*, (January-February).

Lewis, G. 1968. *The Growth of the Modern West Indies*, London: McGibbon and Kee.

Lewis, V. 1984. "Geopolitical Realities in the Caribbean" in *Perspectives on Caribbean Identity,* edited by E. Thomas-Hope. Liverpool: University of Liverpool, Centre for Latin American Studies.

_____. 1987. "The Organization Mission" in *OECS in Perspective 1987,* Castries, Saint Lucia: OECS Secretariat.

Lewis, W.A. 1950. "The Industrialization of the British West Indies", *Caribbean Economic Review* 2 (1).

_____. 1965. *The Agony of the Eight*, Bridgetown: *Barbados Advocate*, Commercial Printing.

Lowenthal, D. 1984. "An Island is a World: The Problem of Caribbean Insularity" in *Perspectives on Caribbean Identity*, edited by E. Thomas-Hope. Liverpool: University of Liverpool, Centre for Latin American Studies.

Macridis, R. 1980. *Contemporary Political Ideologies*, Cambridge, Mass: Withrop.

Manley, M. 1970. "Overcoming Insularity in Jamaica", *Foreign Affairs* 49 (1): 100-10.

Manley, N. 1948. Speech delivered at the Conference on the Closer Assocation of the British West Indies Colonies, 11-19 September 1947, Montego Bay (Jamaica). London: H.M. Stationery Office (Gt. Britain, Parliament, Papers by Command, Cmd. 7291, PE 2, Colonial 218).

McIntyre, A. 1984. "Review of Integration Movements in the Third World with Particular Reference to the Caribbean Community" in *Ten Years of CARICOM*, Washington D.C.

Millette, J. 1969. Review of "The West Indies: The Federal Negotiations", by J. Mordecai. *Social and Economic Studies* 18:408-20.

Mordecai, J. 1963. *The West Indies: The Federal Negotiations*, London: George Allen and Unwin.

Naipual, V.S. 1969. *The Mimic Men*, Harmondsworth: Penguin Books.

Nettleford, R. 1978. *Caribbean Cultural Identity: The Case of Jamaica*, Kingston: Institute of Jamaica.

Payne, A. 1980. *The Politics of the Caribbean Community 1961-79*, Manchester: Manchester University Press.

Proctor, J. 1964. *Constitutional Defeats and the Collapse of the West Indies Federation*, Durham, N.C.: Duke University, Commonwealth Studies Centre. Reprint *Public Law* (Summer).

Reubens, E.P. 1962. *Migration and Development in the West Indies*, Mona, Jamaica: ISER.

Samuel, W. 1987. "The Integration Experience in the Caribbean Common Market". Paper presented at the First Conference of Caribbean Economists, 2-6 July, Jamaica.

Sandiford, E. 1988. *Speeches, June 1987-May 1988*, Bridgetown: Barbados Government Information Service.

Searle, C. 1983. *Grenada: The Struggle Against Destabilization*, n.p., Writers and Readers Publishing Corporation.

Seawar, L. 1988. "Foreign Policy Decision-making in the Commonwealth Caribbean", *Caribbean Affairs* 1(1), January-March.

Spinelli, H. 1974. "The Growth of the European Movement since the Second World War", in *European Integration*, edited by M. Hodges. Harmondsworth: Penguin Books.

Springer, H. 1962. *Reflections on the Failure of the West Indies Federation*, Cambridge, Mass: Harvard University, Centre for International Affairs.

Stephens, S., and D. Stephens. 1986. *Democratic Socialism in Jamaica*, London: Macmillan Educational.

Ten Years of CARICOM. 1984. Washington D.C.

Thomas, C.Y. 1975. *On Formulating a Marxist Theory of Regional Integration*, Georgetown: University of Guyana, mimeo.

—————. 1979. "Neo-colonialism and Caribbean Integration" in *Contemporary International Relations in the Caribbean*, edited by B. Ince. Saint Augustine, Trinidad and Tobago: University of the West Indies, Institute for International Relations.

—————. 1984. *The Rise of the Authoritarian State in Peripheral Societies*, New York and London: Monthly Review Press.

Thomas, C.Y., and H. Brewster. 1967. *The Dynamics of West Indian Economic Integration*, Mona, Jamaica: ISER.

Thomas-Hope, E., ed. 1984. *Perspectives on Caribbean Identity,* University of Liverpool: Centre for Latin American Studies.

Time for Action: Report of the West Indian Commission. 1992. Black Rock, Barbados: The West Indian Commission.

Treaty Establishing the Caribbean Community, Chaguaramas, 4th July, 1973. 1973. Georgetown, Guyana: CARICOM Secretariat.

Trinidad Express. 1977. 9 December. Port-of-Spain, Trinidad.

———— . 1978. 12 February. Port-of-Spain, Trinidad.

Tucker, Robert, ed. 1972. *Marx and Engles: Reader,* New York: W.W. Norton and Company Inc.

Villamil, J. 1984. "The Future of the Caribbean: the International Context", in *Perspectives on Caribbean Identity,* edited by E. Thomas-Hope. University of Liverpool: Centre for Latin American Studies.

Weber, M. 1976. *The Protestant Ethic and the Spirit of Capitalism,* New York: Charles Scribner and Sons.

Williams, E. 1956. "Federation: Two Public Lectures", Port-of-Spain, Trinidad: People's National Movement.

———— . 1959. "The Economics of Nationhood", Port-of-Spain, Trinidad: Office of the Prime Minister.

———— . 1965. "Reflections on the Caribbean Economic Community". Reprinted from *The Nation,* 14 September to 11 November.

Wiltshire-Brodber, R. 1984. "What Role do Caribbean People Play in Promoting Regional Integration: Toward a Wholistic Theory of Regional Integration", in *Ten Years of CARICOM,* Washington D.C.